❦ *Pocket* ❦
IRISH WIT
&WISDOM

Gill Books
Hume Avenue, Park West, Dublin 12

www.gillbooks.ie

Gill Books is an imprint of M.H. Gill & Co.

Copyright © Teapot Press Ltd 2016

ISBN: 978-0-7171-6921-4

This book was created and produced by Teapot Press Ltd

Text by Fiona Biggs
Designed by Alyssa Peacock & Tony Potter

Printed in the EU

This book is typeset in Garamond & Dax

A CIP catalogue record for this book is available
from the British Library.

5 4 3 2

Pocket IRISH WIT & WISDOM

Gill Books

Contents

Part 2 – Love and Marriage, Irish-Style

Part 3 – A Curious Custom of Death

Part 4 – Biographies

INTRODUCTION

The Irish have a worldwide reputation for wit. Never renowned for a repertoire of obvious jokes, we have a particular brand of humour that is usually offbeat. We are masterly raconteurs and can take such an oblique approach to sending up a person or a situation that there is often a heartbeat after the delivery of the punch line before the arrow hits its mark. No person or situation is sacrosanct: clergy, lawyers, politicians, government institutions, death, wealth, marriage, religion, taxes – the list of butts is endless.

The redeeming grace of what is sometimes seen as our savage wit is the fact that the jokes are frequently told against ourselves. Perhaps our history has led us to take that peculiarly Irish approach to difficulty and misfortune, allowing us to release the pressure from a difficult moment or situation with an off-the-cuff quip or one-liner. Seán O'Casey once said of us that we 'treat a joke as a serious thing, and a serious thing as a joke'. And perhaps our wisdom lies in our refusal to take everything too seriously – a frequently heard response to a bad situation or event in Ireland is 'sure, it will all be the same 100 years from now'.

This book contains just a small selection from the vast reservoir of Irish wit and wisdom, but you will find within its pages a proverb for every occasion and an abundance of quips and quotes that will have you laughing out loud.

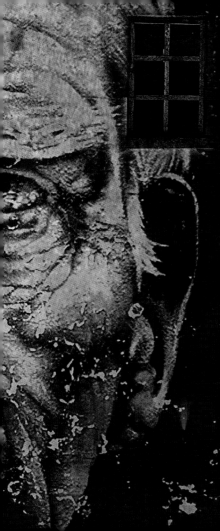

Part 1

That's Life

The hallway of
every man's life
is paced with
pictures; pictures
gay and pictures
gloomy, all useful,
for if we be wise,
we can learn from
them a richer and
braver way to live.

– *Samuel Beckett*

Being Alive

The Irish would be the first to tell you that our difficult history has equipped us to deal with the vagaries of the human condition with a strange mixture of cheerfulness, fortitude, resentment and fatalism. From the positive to the downright cynical, our attitudes to life are mirrored in our wit and wisdom.

The book of life begins with a man and a woman in a garden; it ends with revelations.

– *Oscar Wilde*

Life is no brief candle to me. It is a sort of splendid torch which I have got a hold of for the moment, and I want to make it burn as brightly as possible before handing it on to future generations.

– *George Bernard Shaw*

The only sin is the sin of being born.

– *Samuel Beckett*

To learn one must be humble. But life is the great teacher.

– *James Joyce*

Life is much too important a thing ever to talk seriously about it.

– *Oscar Wilde*

May you live all the days of your life.

– *Jonathan Swift*

You're on earth. There's no cure for that.

– *Samuel Beckett*

Life is a journey that must be travelled, no matter how bad the road and accommodations.

– *Oliver Goldsmith*

Life is a long preparation for something that never happens.

– *W. B. Yeats*

Birth was the death of him.

– *Samuel Beckett*

You can preach a better sermon with your life than with your lips.

— *Oliver Goldsmith*

Life does not cease to be
funny when people die any
more than it ceases to be
serious when people laugh.

George Bernard Shaw

A Child is Born

Irish traditions surrounding the passage into this world were mostly to do with keeping the mother and baby safe, so protective saints were heavily invoked, rosaries were said, and saints' medals and other religious objects were kept at hand. A needle with a broken eye was used to pierce the mother's clothes, in an attempt to alleviate the pain of childbirth.

It was believed that babies born at night before midnight would be able to see ghosts, and if they were born on May Day they would be lucky throughout their lives. It was considered very unlucky for three people in the same family to have a birthday in the same month.

If a baby became sickly after it was born, it was thought to be a changeling, swapped by the fairies for a healthy child. Tying a red ribbon on the cradle or on the child's ankle or wrist was thought to protect against this kidnapping. Salt under the cradle and a piece of iron in the cradle itself were also believed to have protective properties. Empty cradles and rocking chairs were never rocked – the first was thought to curse the child, and the second to curse the mother.

Advice

Easy to give, hard to take, seldom followed.

Good advice has no price.

– Irish proverb

It is always a silly thing to give advice, but to give good advice is absolutely fatal.

– Oscar Wilde

Good advice often comes from a fool.

– Irish proverb

I always pass on good advice – it is the only thing one can do with it.

– Oscar Wilde

Advice is like kissing. It costs nothing and it's a pleasant thing to do.

– George Bernard Shaw

Alcohol

The Irish have an ambivalent relationship with alcohol - we love to drink it, we hate what it does to us. It makes us laugh and it makes us cry, and sometimes it ruins us.

When Saint Patrick first visited Ireland there was no word in the Irish language to express sobriety.

– *Oliver St John Gogarty*

It's the first drop that destroys you – there's no harm at all in the last.

– *Irish saying*

The only cure for drinking is to drink more.

– *Irish saying*

A true Irishman is a fellow who would trample over the bodies of twelve naked women to reach a pint of porter.

– *Seán Ó Faoláin*

An Irishman is never drunk as long as he can hold on to one blade of grass and not fall off the face of the earth.

– *Irish saying*

I am a strict teetotaller, not taking anything between drinks.

– *James Joyce*

Did it ever occur to you that the bottom of a whiskey bottle is much too near to the top?

– *Seán Ó Faoláin*

Drink is the curse of my unhappy country. I take it myself because I have a weak heart and a poor digestion; but in principle I'm a teetotaller.

– *George Bernard Shaw*

The truth comes out when the spirit goes in.

– *Irish proverb*

A tavern is a place where they sell madness by the bottle.

– *Jonathan Swift*

A Catholic priest was preaching a sermon on the dangers of drink to a congregation composed of farm tenants.

'Drink, my dear people, makes you beat your wives, starve your children and shoot your landlords – and it makes you miss them too.'

I attribute my long and healthy life to the fact that I never touched a cigarette, a drink or a girl until I was ten years old.

– *George Moore*

The day the Catholic and Protestant Churches combine, it's the end of all drinking. I'll have to go to Rome and sabotage the affair.

– *Brendan Behan*

A doctor was having trouble making a diagnosis. The patient didn't have any obvious symptoms, but there was clearly something wrong with him.

'I can't work this out at all, Pat,' the doctor said. 'It must be the drink.'

'Never mind, Doctor, I'll come back when you're sober.'

Dreams and Ambitions

What would life be without something to aspire to? Sometimes dreams are the only things that keep us going, although they may not always come true.

We are all in the gutter, but some of us are looking at the stars.

– *Oscar Wilde*

In this world there are only two tragedies; one is not getting what one wants, the other is getting it.

– *Oscar Wilde*

_____

If you take too long in deciding what to do with your life, you'll find you've done it.

– *George Bernard Shaw*

_____

Often has the likely failed and the unlikely succeeded.

– *Irish proverb*

No man can discover his own talents.

– *Brendan Behan*

I have had my hand on the moon; what is the use of trying to rise a little way from the ground?

– *Oscar Wilde*

It is as painful perhaps to be awakened from a vision as to be born.

– *James Joyce*

Glory is fleeting, but obscurity is for ever.

– *George Moore*

The prospect of success in achieving our most cherished dream is not without its terrors. Who is more deprived and alone than the man who has achieved his dream?

– *Brendan Behan*

Every cripple has his own way of walking.

– *Brendan Behan*

Doing what needs to be done may not make you happy, but it will make you great.

– *George Bernard Shaw*

No yesterdays are ever wasted for those who give themselves to today.

– *Brendan Behan*

Every man, through fear, mugs his aspirations a dozen times a day.

– *Brendan Behan*

Success does not consist in never making mistakes but in never making the same one a second time.

– *George Bernard Shaw*

If you accept your limitations you go beyond them.

– *Brendan Behan*

The most important things to do in the world are to get something to eat, something to drink and somebody to love you.

– *Brendan Behan*

Education

Education is greatly valued in Ireland, harking back to the time when the Penal Laws banned Catholic schools and travelling scholars taught in secret outdoor schools.

Examinations consist of the foolish asking questions the wise cannot answer.

– *Oscar Wilde*

Ignorance is a rare, exotic fruit; touch it and the bloom has gone.

– *Oscar Wilde*

_____

Encourage youth and it will prosper.

– *Irish proverb*

_____

Education is an admirable thing, but it is well to remember from time to time that nothing worth knowing can be taught.

– *Oscar Wilde*

Everybody who is incapable of learning has taken to teaching.

– *Oscar Wilde*

Youths and fools are hardest taught.

– *Irish proverb*

There is many a man without learning will get the better of a college-bred man, and will have better words, too.

– *Lady Gregory*

He who can, does. He who cannot, teaches.

– *George Bernard Shaw*

Education is not the filling of a pail, but the lighting of a fire.

– *W. B. Yeats*

Learning is a light load.

– *Irish proverb*

What everyone knows is hardly worth knowing.

– *Irish saying*

Law

As a nation we have a strange relationship with the law – we have scant respect for its institutions and practitioners, yet we are a most litigious race and love to 'have our day in court'.

Law grinds the poor and rich men rule the law.

– Oliver Goldsmith

More bitterness is caused by not making wills than by not making up.

– Irish proverb

I have never seen a situation so dismal that a policeman couldn't make it worse.

– Brendan Behan

The man that is not prejudiced against a horse thief is not fit to sit on a jury in this town.

– George Bernard Shaw

Laws are like cobwebs, which may catch small flies, but let wasps and hornets through.

– Jonathan Swift

Once you attempt legislation upon religious grounds, you open the way for every kind of intolerance and religious persecution.

– *W. B. Yeats*

If the Church and the devil went to law the devil would win, for all the lawyers and attorneys would be on his side.

– *Jonathan Swift*

Only lawyers and mental defectives are automatically exempt from jury duty.

– *George Bernard Shaw*

The right to pay fees to lawyers is an ancient and fundamental human right, and is at the kernel of what we know as democracy.

– *Flann O'Brien*

It is a maxim among these lawyers, that whatever hath been done before, may legally be done again: and therefore they take special care to record all the decisions formerly made against common justice and the general reason of mankind.

– *Jonathan Swift*

'You're a fine sort of fellow, aren't you?' said the prosecuting barrister to the defence witness.

'I'd say the same about you,' was the reply. 'Only I'm under oath.'

The lawyer John Philpot Curran was out riding with a judge who was renowned for his harsh sentencing.

'Where would you be, Curran, if that scaffold had its due?' asked the judge as they passed a gallows.

'Riding alone, my lord,' Curran replied.

'And what is your verdict?' the judge asked the foreman of the jury.

'We find the man who stole the horse not guilty, your honour.'

'Who is representing you?' the judge asked the defendant.

'I'm representing myself, your honour.'

'Well, then how are you pleading? Guilty or not guilty?'

'Not guilty, of course, your honour. If I was guilty I'd have a lawyer.'

Brehon Law

Before the English system of common law supplanted it in the 17th century, the Irish administered a system of justice that was known as Brehon law. Cases were decided by arbitrators rather than judges – unusually, capital punishment was not one of the penalties available, even in cases of murder. Crimes were usually punishable with fines, which were paid in restitution to the victims.

In many ways Brehon law was very progressive – divorce was available and men and women had equal rights. There was no formal system of courts in place and there was no police force. Perhaps the ancient Irish were law-abiding types?

English law began to seep into the fabric of Irish society in the late 12th century, but was confined to the Pale until the 1500s, when Henry VIII extended it further into the country. By the early 1600s, Brehon law had been superseded by the common law of England.

'You're working very hard these days, Brigid,' said Mary, when she came upon her friend struggling through the door with yet another load of laundry.

'I am, that,' panted Brigid, as she wrestled with the fine linen sheets. 'I've been taking in more washing since the judge ordered me to keep the peace after I went for that Susan Lynch down the road and tore some of her hair out.'

'So all the extra work keeps you busy and out of her way? asked Mary.

'It does, surely, but that's not the point. I'm saving up the fine for the next time.'

A repeat offender was brought before the judge

'Here again?' asked the judge. 'What's brought you here this time?'

'Those two policemen, your honour,' said the defendant, pointing to the two officers on either side of him.

'I know that,' said the judge impatiently. 'Drunk again, I suppose?'

'Yes, your honour. The both of them.'

A bailiff was ordered to clear the court.

'Would all you blackguards who aren't lawyers please leave the court!' he shouted.

Money

We need it to live, but it causes no end of problems.

It's harder to gather than to scatter.

– *Irish proverb*

It's a grand thing to be able to take money in your hand and to think no more of it when it slips away from you than you would a trout that would slip back into the stream.

– *Lady Gregory*

Where wealth accumulates, men decay.

– *Oliver Goldsmith*

It's better to be born lucky than to be born rich.

– *Irish proverb*

Forgetting a debt doesn't pay it.

– *Irish proverb*

A cheque is the only argument I recognise.

– *Oscar Wilde*

A poor man never lost his property.

– *Irish proverb*

They're so mean they'd give you one measle at a time.

– *Irish saying*

_____

He's so tight he still has his First Communion money.

– *Irish saying*

_____

Money borrowed is soon sorrowed.

– *Irish proverb*

_____

Money is a good servant but a bad master.

– *Irish proverb*

A man cannot grow rich without his wife's leave.

– *Irish proverb*

_____

Anyone who lives within their means suffers from a lack of imagination.

– *Oscar Wilde*

When I was young I thought that money was the most important thing in life; now I know it is.

– *George Bernard Shaw*

Nothing is so hard for those who abound in riches as to conceive how others can be in want.

– *Jonathan Swift*

You don't have to live with the man you cheat, but you do have to live with your conscience.

– *Irish proverb*

A wise man should have money in his head but not in his heart.

– *Jonathan Swift*

It is better to have a permanent income than to be fascinating.

– *Oscar Wilde*

Short accounts make long friends.

– *Irish proverb*

Money does not make you happy but it quiets the nerves.

– *Samuel Beckett*

Better to go to bed hungry than rise from it in debt.

– *Irish proverb*

I never refuse money. I come from a family where it was considered unlucky to refuse money.

– *Patrick Kavanagh*

Young people nowadays assume that money is everything, and when they get older they know it.

– *Oscar Wilde*

Politics

The issue of politics is very close to the hearts of the Irish. Our attitude towards politicians is an odd combination of respect and loathing.

He knows nothing; and he thinks he knows everything. That points clearly to a political career.

– *George Bernard Shaw*

A government which robs Peter to pay Paul can always depend on the support of Paul.

– *George Bernard Shaw*

A man should always be drunk when he talks politics – it's the only way in which to make them important.

– *Seán O'Casey*

All political parties die of swallowing their own lies.

– *Jonathan Swift*

Paddy was walking through a graveyard when he came across a headstone with the inscription, 'Here lies a politician and an honest man.' He scratched his head, puzzled.

'I wonder how they managed to get the two of them into the one grave.'

And he gave it for his opinion, that whoever could make two ears of corn, or two blades of grass, to grow upon a spot of ground where only one grew before, would deserve better of mankind, and do more essential service to his country, than the whole race of politicians put together.

– *Jonathan Swift*

When my son Tom announced that he would claim his independence of party as MP by writing the words TO LET on his forehead, I advised him to write underneath, UNFURNISHED.

– *Richard Brinsley Sheridan*

The street was in a rough neighbourhood. It was near the Houses of Parliament.

– *Oscar Wilde*

The only man who had a proper understanding of Parliament was old Guy Fawkes.

– *George Bernard Shaw*

A [political party] is the madness of many for the gain of a few.

– *Jonathan Swift*

Relationships

Other people – we need them, but they can drive us mad.

It is always painful to part from people whom one has known for a very brief space of time. The absence of old friends one can endure with equanimity.

– *Oscar Wilde*

Always forgive your enemies. Nothing annoys them so much.

– *Oscar Wilde*

It is very easy to endure the difficulties of one's enemies. It is the successes of one's friends that are hard to bear.

– *Oscar Wilde*

Blood is thicker than water and easier seen.

– *Irish saying*

No man ever wore a scarf as warm as his daughter's arm around his neck.

– *Irish saying*

The family without a skeleton in the cupboard has it buried.

– *Irish saying*

What really flatters a man is that you think him worth flattering.

– *George Bernard Shaw*

Do not do unto others as you would they should do unto you. Their tastes may not be the same.

– *George Bernard Shaw*

Religion

The thorny subject of religion is always up for discussion in Ireland.

I'm an atheist and I thank God for it.

– *George Bernard Shaw*

The Catholic Church is for saints and sinners. For respectable people the Anglican Church will do.

– *Oscar Wilde*

Religion is the fashionable substitute for belief.

– *Oscar Wilde*

The want of belief is a defect that ought to be concealed when it cannot be overcome.

– *Jonathan Swift*

Irish atheists have started a Dial-A-Prayer service; when you ring them, nobody answers.

– *Hal Roach*

No man ever believes that the Bible means what it says: He is always convinced that it says what he means.

– *George Bernard Shaw*

I cannot stand Christians because they are never Catholics and I cannot stand Catholics because they are never Christians. Otherwise I am at one with the Indivisible Church.

– Oscar Wilde

He is such a devout Catholic he won't be happy until he's crucified.

– John B. Keane

What's the Ascendancy? A Protestant on a horse.

– Brendan Behan

There is no heresy or no philosophy which is so abhorrent to the church as a human being.

– James Joyce

Some people say there is a God; others say there is no God. The truth probably lies somewhere in between.

– W. B. Yeats

Get on your knees and thank God you're still on your feet.

– Irish saying

Communism is the lay form of Catholicism.

– *George Bernard Shaw*

I never saw, heard, nor read, that the clergy were beloved in any nation where Christianity was the religion of the country. Nothing can render them popular but some degree of persecution.

– *Jonathan Swift*

I don't have any religion – I am an Irish Protestant.

– *Oscar Wilde*

An Irish Protestant asked a Catholic priest what he thought about Purgatory.

'Well,' came the reply, 'it's my belief you could go further and do a lot worse.'

Become a Protestant? Certainly not. Just because I've lost my faith doesn't mean I've lost my reason.

– *James Joyce*

When the gods want to punish us they answer our prayers.

– *Oscar Wilde*

Jamesie brought a newborn kitten to the local vicar and asked him to buy it.

'You should have it, Your Reverence,' he said. 'It's a good Protestant kitten.'

The vicar refused, so the following week Jamesie tried his luck with the parish priest.

'It's a good Catholic kitten, Father,' he said. 'You could give it a good home.'

'Go on out of that, Jamesie,' replied the priest. 'I heard you only last week telling the vicar it was a good Protestant.'

'That's true,' said Jamesie. 'But that was before its eyes were opened.'

When I'm in health I'm not at all religious. But when I'm sick I'm very religious.

– *Brendan Behan*

I never knew any man in my life who could not bear another's misfortune perfectly like a Christian.

– *Jonathan Swift*

What would I like the sermon to be about? I would like it be about ten minutes.

– *Arthur Wellesley, Duke of Wellington*

Irish Protestantism is not a religion. It is a class prejudice, a conviction that Roman Catholics are socially inferior persons who will go to Hell when they die and leave Heaven in the exclusive possession of Protestant ladies and gentlemen.

– *George Bernard Shaw*

I am somewhat surprised to hear a Roman Catholic quote so essentially Protestant a document as the Bible.

– *George Bernard Shaw*

Sport

Sport, that great national pastime – or is it?

Games are for people who can neither read nor think.

– *George Bernard Shaw*

Football is all very well – a good game for rough girls, but not delicate boys.

– *Oscar Wilde*

Golf is the only game in the world in which a precise knowledge of the rules can earn you a reputation for bad sportsmanship.

– *Patrick Campbell*

I never play cricket. It requires one to assume such indecent postures.

– *Oscar Wilde*

A businessman is someone to whom age brings golf rather than wisdom.

– *George Bernard Shaw*

I detest games – I never like to kick or be kicked.

– *Oscar Wilde*

The best hurlers are those on the ditch.

– *Irish proverb*

If he bet on the tide, it wouldn't come in for him.

– *Irish saying*

Baseball has the advantage over cricket of being sooner ended.

– *George Bernard Shaw*

In baseball I see no reason why the infield should not try to put the batter off his stride at the critical moment by neatly timed disparagement of his mother's respectability.

– *George Bernard Shaw*

The spectacle of twenty-two grown men with hairy legs chasing a bladder filled with air from one end of a field to another is both ludicrous and infantile.

– *George Bernard Shaw*

Joe and Paddy went to the races and they each placed a bet on a seven-horse race. As the horses appeared, they both started getting excited.

'Where's mine?' Joe asked Paddy, who by this time was jumping up and down, shouting at the horses as they galloped towards the finish line.

'I don't know,' came the reply. 'I'm only watching the first six.'

Wisdom and Experience

Wisdom is supposed to come with age, but does our experience of life really make us any wiser?

Age makes you weaker but wiser.

– *Irish proverb*

No man was ever so completely skilled in the conduct of life, as not to receive new information from age and experience.

– *Jonathan Swift*

You don't stop laughing when you grow old, you grow old when you stop laughing.

– *George Bernard Shaw*

Only a fool wouldn't get value from a borrowed horse.

– *Irish proverb*

Experience is the name everyone gives to their mistakes.

– *Oscar Wilde*

Folly rides for a fall.

– *Irish proverb*

We're not the men our fathers were. If we were we'd be terribly old.

– *Flann O'Brien*

The wearer knows best where the boot pinches.

– *Irish proverb*

Try again. Fail again. Fail better.

– *Samuel Beckett*

Never call a man a fool until you're sure he's not a rogue.

– *Irish proverb*

No wise man ever wished to be younger.

– *Jonathan Swift*

Empty heads keep open mouths.

– *Irish proverb*

My mistakes are my life.

– *Samuel Beckett*

Youth is wasted on the young.

– *George Bernard Shaw*

Every man is wise till he speaks.

– *Irish proverb*

Work

Love it or loathe it, we all need to work. The Irish have an unfounded reputation for being lazy; perhaps it's because we're always complaining about our jobs (but that doesn't mean they don't get done).

A job is death without the dignity.

— *Brendan Behan*

A foot at rest gets little spun.

— *Irish proverb*

Well begun is the job half done.

— *Irish proverb*

If you'd prefer to be doing something else, you're working.

— *Irish saying*

Work is the curse of the drinking classes.

— *Oscar Wilde*

The only really dirty four-lettered word is 'work'.

— *Brendan Kennelly*

A busy mother makes an idle daughter.

– *Irish proverb*

They were a people so primitive they did not know how to get money except by working for it.

– *Joseph Addison*

Work is the refuge of people who have nothing better to do.

– *Oscar Wilde*

The only thing that has to be finished by next Friday is next Thursday.

– *Maureen Potter*

The lazy man says he can always be busy tomorrow.

– *Irish saying*

Results come not by chance but through hard work.

– *Irish proverb*

You'll never plough a field by turning it over in your mind.

— *Irish proverb*

People who say manual labour is a good thing have never done any.

— *Brendan Behan*

A man was hard at work digging a drain for his new house. Two of his friends came by and started chatting to him while he worked. A local judge saw the crossed the road to see what was going on.

'Typical,' he said. 'One man working and the other two looking on idly.'

'That'd be three men looking on idly, your honour,' said the digger, with a smile.

There was a malfunction in a sewer and a team of workers were sent down to repair it. The foreman arrived two hours later, stood at the edge of the manhole and shouted down:

'How many men are down there?'

'There's three of us here, boss,' was the reply.

'Well, let half of you come back up,' the foreman ordered.

A Few Proverbs on Life and Living

Don't throw away the sweepings of the bag until you check if you dropped your ring into it.

Never trust a fine day in winter, the life of an old man, or an important person's word – unless it's in writing.

There's no stopping the force of a moving wheel.

Don't cross the man who was reared without shoes – his feet will be hard from walking over people.

As the old cock crows, the young cock learns.

The last horse home blames the bit.

Borrowed time
brings no interest.

Better an old hat than
a borrowed one.

What is in the
dog comes out
in the pup.

The smaller the cottage,
the wider the door.

A charitable man
has never gone
to hell.

If you never come up in
this world, you won't go
down in the next.

What you don't have you
can't miss.

I need her company as
much as a headache needs
noise.

The man with sense doesn't talk before breakfast.

It's best to travel slowly on an unknown road.

Never promise a fish until it's caught.

Leave the bad news where you found it.

A friend's eye is the best mirror.

A watched pot never boils.

Bad luck sends no warning.

The latest misfortune is the greatest misfortune.

The sun shines brightest after the rain.

Better half a loaf than no bread at all.

Every tide has its ebb.

However long the day, it ends with night.

A sense of humour is no burden, but it makes heavy loads easier to carry.

Every patient is a doctor after his cure.

The whole world could not make a racehorse out of a donkey.

Buried embers may turn to flames.

The greedy man hoards everything except friendship.

Neither make nor break a custom.

A kind word never broke a tooth.

One rogue recognises another.

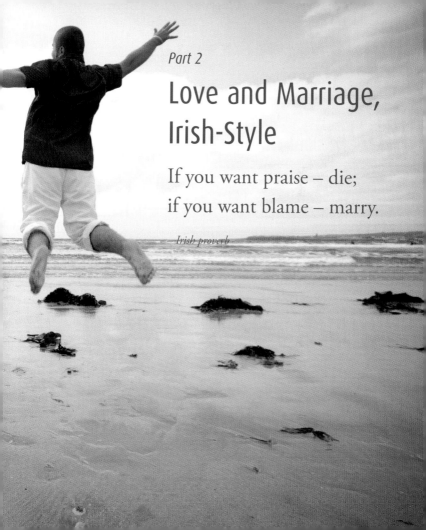

Part 2

Love and Marriage, Irish-Style

If you want praise – die;
if you want blame – marry.

Irish proverb

A Great Institution

It is said that if you marry in haste you'll repent at leisure, and there is probably no subject that has produced more cynical jokes and more wise and witty aphorisms than the topic of love (and marriage). As these have generally been penned or uttered by men, it is usually women who bear the brunt of things.

I have never seen a woman for whom I would give up the middle of the bed.

– *Jonathan Swift*

Good heavens! How marriage ruins a man! It's as demoralising as cigarettes and far more expensive.

– *Oscar Wilde*

The honest man who married and brought up a large family, did more service than he who continued single and only talked of population.

– *Oliver Goldsmith*

I wonder what fool it was that first invented kissing?

– Jonathan Swift

Friendship is a disinterested commerce between equals; love, an abject intercourse between tyrants and slaves.

– Oliver Goldsmith

Rich bachelors should be taxed. It is not fair that some men should be happier than others.

– Oscar Wilde

I have known more men destroyed by the desire to have wife and child and to keep them in comfort than I have seen destroyed by drink and harlots.

– W. B. Yeats

Bigamy is having one wife/husband too many. Monogamy is the same.

– Oscar Wilde

Marriage is popular because it combines the maximum of temptation with the maximum of opportunity.

– George Bernard Shaw

Venus, a beautiful, good-natured lady, was the goddess of love; Juno, a terrible shrew, the goddess of marriage; and they were always mortal enemies.

– *George Bernard Shaw*

Dammit, sir, it is your duty to get married. You can't always be living for pleasure.

– *Oscar Wilde*

The real drawback of marriage is that it makes one unselfish.

– *Oscar Wilde*

If there were no husbands, who would look after our mistresses?

– *George Moore*

Marriage is an alliance entered into by a man who can't sleep with the window shut, and a woman who can't sleep with the window open.

– *George Bernard Shaw*

Confusing monogamy with morality has done more to destroy the conscience of the human race than any other error.

– *George Bernard Shaw*

If I had not married I should not have learned the quick enrichment of sentences that one gets in conversation; had I not been widowed I should not have found the detachment of mind, the leisure for observation necessary to give insight into character, to express and interpret it. Loneliness made me rich.

– Lady Gregory

Love and Courtship

Through the ages, it has always been the few weeks and months following Cupid's first strike that are celebrated in songs and poetry. The wise and witty have always taken a slightly more jaundiced view of the whole business of romantic love. The man is usually presented as a 'catch' and the woman as a calculating husband-hunter, taking advantage of the less wily male of the species.

First love is only a little foolishness and a lot of curiosity. No really self-respecting woman would take advantage of it.

– *George Bernard Shaw*

I would rather choose a wife of mine to have the usual number of limbs, and although one eye may be very agreeable, the prejudice has always run in favour of two.

– *Richard Brinsley Sheridan*

If a man is in love he is no judge of beauty, but when love wears off he'll tell her about her warts.

– *George Bernard Shaw*

The real genius for love lies not in getting into, but getting out of love.

– *George Moore*

If you love her in rags, your love will last.

– *Irish proverb*

When we want to read about the deeds that are done for love, whither do we turn? To the murder columns.

– *George Bernard Shaw*

You'll only see the faults of a beautiful woman if you close your eyes.

– *Irish proverb*

If she pleases the eye, she'll please the heart.

– *Irish proverb*

A woman seeking a husband is the most unscrupulous of all beasts of prey.

– George Bernard Shaw

A man is already half in love with any woman who listens to him.

– Brendan Behan

A woman waits motionless until she is wooed. That is how the spider waits for the fly.

– George Bernard Shaw

Love is intoxicating – it pleases at first, then sends its victim reeling.

– Irish proverb

Would you like to be buried with my people?

– Irish marriage proposal

Life is one fool thing after another, whereas love is two fool things after each other.

– Oscar Wilde

Paddy and Julia met for the first time after their parents had struck a satisfactory bargain for the marriage of their offspring.

'Why didn't you tell me she was lame?' hissed Paddy, when Julia limped into the house.

'Sure, why would we? It's not for running races you want her!' retorted his father.

His Goose is Cooked

Until the last century, matchmaking was a very serious business in Ireland. Arranged, or 'must', marriages were a popular way of making sure that young people married and had children, carrying on the family name. The eldest girl in a family was the first to be married, and her sisters then had matches arranged for them in order of age. Usually, the engaged couple had known each other all their lives, although occasionally an elderly widower or bachelor was matched with a young woman. The parents agreed all the terms of the dowry and the matchmaker (usually a man) received a bottle of whiskey for his trouble. The bride's parents were invited to 'walk the land' of the groom's family, so they could see for themselves how much property was being brought to the table. When a deal was struck, it could not be cancelled without enormous loss of face. To seal the deal, the bride's family invited the groom's family (and everyone else involved in the wedding) for a meal of roast goose, which gave rise to the expression 'his goose is cooked'.

Play with the woman that has beauty; marry the woman that has property.

– *Irish proverb*

Don't make a bid until you walk the land.

– *Irish proverb*

Many an Irish property was increased by the lace of a daughter's petticoat.

– *Irish proverb*

His Goose is Cooked

Of course, no matter how careful the parents, some couples jumped the gun. In some parts of Ireland a man would go to the house of the woman he wanted to marry and throw his cap through the front door. If it was thrown out again, she wasn't interested.

'Come, come,' said Tom's father,
'At your time of life,
There's no longer excuse
For thus playing the rake.
It is time you should think, boy,
Of taking a wife.'

'Why, so it is, Father –
Whose wife shall I take?'

– *Thomas Moore*

Leap Year Opportunity

There's an old Irish legend that St Brigid and St Patrick, concerned about some men's reluctance to marry and settle down, agreed that women should be allowed to propose to men once every four years. A female proposal had to be made on 29 February, when Leap Day balances the calendar every four years. If a man refused the proposal, the forfeit was a silk gown for the proposer.

I chose my wife, as she did her wedding gown, for qualities that would wear well.

– *Oliver Goldsmith*

A man who says his wife can't take a joke forgets that she took him.

– *Oscar Wilde*

Women love men for their defects; if men have enough of them, women will forgive them anything, even their gigantic intellects.

– *Oscar Wilde*

Women are so enigmatical – some in everything – all in matters of the heart. Don't they sometimes actually admire what is repulsive?

– *Joseph Sheridan Le Fanu*

A flicker that warms is better than a blaze that burns.

– *Irish proverb*

Keep your eyes open before you get married and half shut afterwards.

– *Irish proverb*

The Claddagh Ring

The Claddagh ring – a crowned heart held by two hands – is well known around the world as a symbol of enduring love. This traditional ring comes from County Galway, in the small coastal area known as the Claddagh. Traditionally, it was handed down from mother to daughter; nowadays it is also given by young men to their girlfriends. It's considered unlucky to buy a Claddagh ring for yourself.

While the ring is clearly a token of love, different ways of wearing it signify different things.

Single women wear the ring on the ring finger of the right hand, the narrow end of the heart pointing outwards, to show that they are available. Women in a steady relationship turn the ring inwards on that same finger, to show that their heart is taken.

When the woman gets engaged, the ring is moved to the left hand, the narrow end of heart pointing outwards. After the wedding, the ring is turned inwards on that finger, never to be moved again.

'But why won't you marry me, Sheila?' begged Tom. 'There isn't anyone else, is there?' he asked suspiciously.

'Oh, Tom,' sighed Sheila. 'I really hope there is.'

Long engagements give people the opportunity of finding out each other's character before marriage, which is never advisable.

– *Oscar Wilde*

An engagement is hardly a serious one that has not been broken off at least once.

– *Oscar Wilde*

Marry the right woman and there's nothing like it; marry the wrong woman and there's nothing like it.

– *Irish saying*

You, that are going to be married, think things can never be done too fast.

– *Oliver Goldsmith*

Getting Married

Weddings in Ireland are a combination of ancient Celtic tradition and modern customs.

Tying the knot

This well-known expression, now an informal description of the marriage ceremony, originates in an old Celtic tradition that predates the Christian sacrament of marriage. The symbolism is clear – the couple being married clasped each other's hands at the point in the ceremony where they made a binding commitment to each other. A cord or ribbon was tied around their joined hands, showing their willingness to spend the rest of their lives bound together as one. This 'handfasting' was part of the civil marriage ceremony. With the advent of Christianity and the move from secular to religious unions, this part of the marriage ceremony was replaced by the exchange of rings, symbolising love without end.

A priest was attempting to marry a young couple at the altar, but the groom was so drunk that he kept falling over.

'I can't marry you with him in this state,' he said to the bride. 'Come back again when he's sober.'

'But Father,' she wept, 'he won't agree to it when he's sober!'

Under this window in stormy weather
I marry this man and woman together;
Let none but Him who rules the thunder
Put this man and woman asunder.

– *Jonathan Swift*

A Few Wedding Day Traditions and Superstitions

When it comes to weddings, Ireland is no different from other cultures in having a long list of traditions and superstitions, not to be disregarded lightly. The universal tradition of the groom not being allowed to see the bride on their wedding day until she arrives at the church is a given – others might seem more unusual.

Take steps to avoid running into a funeral procession on your way to the church. If you do see one coming towards you, turn back and take a different route.

Make sure that the first person to wish you luck is a man.

A bride should never put her veil on herself, and she should make sure that the woman putting it on for her is happily married.

A sunny day for a wedding is a good omen – if the bride looks at the sun when she leaves the house, she will have beautiful children.

If the statue of the Child of Prague is put outside the night before the wedding, the sun will shine on the bride.

An accidental tear in the wedding dress is very lucky, but don't wear anything green on your wedding day. Wear something old, something new, something borrowed, something blue … and carry an old sixpence for luck.

It's lucky for the bride to be woken up by the dawn chorus on the morning of her wedding day and to see a cuckoo first thing; three magpies is also a good omen for a bride.

If someone throws an old shoe over the bride's head as she leaves the church, the marriage will be happy.

May you live to be a hundred years, with one extra year to repent!

– *Irish proverb*

Marry in May, and you'll rue the day;

Marry in April if you can, joy for the maiden and for the man.

– *Irish proverb*

Take a different route on your way back from the church after the wedding – this means you're stepping out on a new road together. This different route should be longer than the one you took to the church.

May your pockets be heavy and your heart be light,

May good luck pursue you each morning and night.

A Few Blessings for the Happy Couple

Health and long life to you,
Land without rent to you,
A child every year to you.
And if you can't go to Heaven,
At least may you die in Ireland!

May there always be work
For your hands to do;
May your purse always hold a coin or two;
May the sun always shine on your window pane;
May a rainbow be certain to follow each rain;
May the hand of a friend always be near you
May God fill your heart with gladness and cheer you.

Walls for the wind, and
a roof for the rain, and
drinks beside the fire.

Laughter to cheer you and
those you love near you,
and all that your heart
may desire!

May your troubles
be less and your
blessings be more.

And nothing but
happiness come
through your door.

And They Lived Happily Ever After ...

There's a good reason why all the fairy tales end with this line! Married life seems to have more difficulties and pitfalls than any other human relationship. According to tradition, the battle between the sexes begins in earnest as soon as the honeymoon is over.

The ideal marriage consists of a deaf husband and a blind wife.

– *Padraic Colum*

All that a husband or wife wants is to be pitied a little, praised a little and appreciated a little.

– *Oliver Goldsmith*

How I wish that Adam had died with all his bones in his body!

– *Dion Boucicault*

There are three kinds of men who can't understand women: young men, old men and middle-aged men.

– *Irish proverb*

'That wife of mine is driving me to drink,' complained Donal.

'Aren't you the lucky one,' said Seán. 'Mine makes me take the bus.'

I'm hoarse listening to my wife complaining.

– Brendan Behan

A quarrelsome married couple came to the parish priest seeking marriage counselling. They could agree on nothing, it seemed. Whatever one said, the other contradicted, and the priest couldn't get a word in edgeways.

'Shame on you,' the priest said, when they had paused for breath at last. 'Your cat and dog get on better than the two of you!'

'That may be, Father,' said the husband. 'But just try tying them together and see what happens.'

Many years ago, in the days of dedicated smoking carriages in trains, a woman boarded a train, entered a smoking compartment and looked pointedly at the man seated at the window who was peaceably smoking his pipe. He took no notice, so she opened the window, sat down and started coughing loudly.

When the man still took no notice and continued to puff out clouds of smoke, the woman glared at him and said:

'If you were my husband, I'd poison you.'

The man looked at her reflectively, then he took the pipe out of his mouth.

'Is that so?' he responded mildly. 'Well, if I were your husband, I'd take it.'

Niagara Falls is the bride's second great disappointment.

– *Oscar Wilde*

The happiness of a married man depends on the people he has not married.

– *Oscar Wilde*

'Tis safest in matrimony to begin with a little aversion.

– *Richard Brinsley Sheridan*

Women want other women's husbands like horse thieves prefer a horse that is broken in to one that is wild.

– *George Bernard Shaw*

Married life is merely a habit.

– *Oscar Wilde*

In married life three is company and two is none.

– *Oscar Wilde*

A wise woman will always let her husband have his way.

– *Richard Brinsley Sheridan*

There is nothing in the world like the devotion of a married woman. It's a thing no married man knows anything about.

– *Oscar Wilde*

'How are you, Mary?' asked Eileen. 'You look exhausted!'

'Ah well, I have my work cut out for me between looking after the fire and that good-for-nothing husband of mine. If I take my eyes off one of them, the other one is sure to go out.'

The world has grown suspicious of anything that looks like a happily married life.

– *Oscar Wilde*

The Effects of Age

Does the sap rise more slowly as we get older? George Moore certainly thought so, and was very precise as to the age at which this decline sets in:

At forty-six or thereabouts one begins to feel that one's time for love is over; one is consultant rather than practitioner.

However, for some, age brings definite advantages and there are many proverbs and quotes to prove it.

The older the fiddle, the sweeter the tune.

– *Irish proverb*

Old coals are easiest kindled.

– *Irish proverb*

The old pipe gives the sweetest smoke.

– *Irish proverb*

Better an old man's darling than a young man's slave.

– *Irish proverb*

Men come of age at sixty, women at sixteen.

– *James Stephens*

There's one good thing
about a late marriage –
it doesn't last long.

– Irish saying

Women delight in men
over seventy. They offer
the devotion of a lifetime.

– Oscar Wilde

Cries Celia to a reverend dean
'What reason can be given
Since marriage is a holy thing,
that there are none in Heaven?'

'There are no women,' he replied;
she quick returned the jest;
'Women there are, but I'm afraid,
They cannot find a priest.'

– John Winstanley

Part 3

A Curious Custom of Death

It is impossible that anything so natural, so necessary, and so universal as death, should ever have been designed by providence as an evil to mankind.

→ *Jonathan Swift*

Agus Bás in Éireann

This is the tail end of an Irish toast that means, literally, 'May you die in Ireland'. It might seem strange to those who are not natives of this island. Perhaps we all want to die here because if there's one thing we do really well, it's death. Far from being something that is hidden away and not spoken of, death is something that is, if not quite embraced, is certainly seen as part of the cycle of life.

– Brendan Behan

Many a day
shall we rest
in the clay.

– Irish proverb

No man is so old
as to believe he
cannot live one
year more.

– Sean O'Casey

May the Good Lord
take a liking to you,
but not too soon.

– Irish blessing

The best words any man can hear at his funeral are 'Carry on with the coffin. The corpse will walk.'

– Brendan Behan

Old persons are sometimes as unwilling to die as tired-out children are to say good night and go to bed.

– Sheridan Le Fanu

Death looks the old in the face and lurks behind the young.

– Irish proverb

Death is the poor man's doctor.

– Irish proverb

There is no bad publicity – except an obituary notice.

– Brendan Behan

If I was dead, I wouldn't know I was dead. That's the only thing I have against death. I want to enjoy my death.

– Samuel Beckett

A Touch of Irreverence

No matter where you go in Ireland, you won't go long without hearing a few irreverent references to death. The levity with which the subject is approached may seem shocking, but it's just our way of dealing with the inevitable, an attempt to conquer our fear of mortality.

I shall never make a new friend in life, though I rather hope to make a few in death.

– *Oscar Wilde*

I don't know if he is dead or not, but they took the liberty of burying him.

– *J. M. Synge*

My grandmother made dying her life's work.

– *Hugh Leonard*

I find if I don't die in autumn, I always seem to survive until Christmas.

– *Richard Brinsley Sheridan*

If you don't know where you are currently standing, you're dead.

– Samuel Beckett

One can survive anything nowadays except death.

– Oscar Wilde

'Tell me,' asked an American visitor at the bar of the village pub. 'Who's the oldest resident of your village?'

'Ah well,' was the barman's reply, 'it's like this. We don't have one any more – he went and died last week.'

'How's Paddy doing?' asked Mary when she met Sheila at the butcher's. 'I heard he was very ill.'

'He was right there at death's door only yesterday,' said Sheila, 'and then that new doctor pulled him through.'

One cold winter's morning, the doctor's waiting room, as usual, was heaving. Hours went by and the number of people didn't seem to diminish, so an old man hauled himself up on his walking sticks and made for the door.

'Where are you off to?' shouted the receptionist. 'You can't just leave – you're on the doctor's list for this morning!'

'I'm off home to die a natural death,' the old man replied as the door closed behind him.

A visitor to a small Irish village was walking along the empty main street. He met an old man and complimented him on the prettiness of the village and said that it seemed to be a very quiet and uneventful little place. 'Indeed it is,' said the old man. 'Sure, we haven't buried a living soul here in years!'

———————————

'It's always puzzled me,' said Joseph, looking up from the death notices in his daily newspaper, 'how God manages to work it out so well. I've been looking at these notices every day for years, and people always seem to die in alphabetical order.'

Paddy the farm labourer was leaning against the wall, looking out into the distance. 'Lazing again, Paddy?' said the farmer as he drove into the yard. 'Sure, you'd be a great messenger to send out looking for Death.'

Heaven and Hell

Alongside the subject of death, the afterlife has always been an Irish preoccupation. Heaven and hell – particularly hell – feature largely in the national repertoire of jokes and proverbs. The devil and St Peter make many an appearance as familiar acquaintances.

May you be in heaven half an hour before the devil knows you are dead.

– Irish blessing

A priest came to give James the last rites as he lay on his deathbed.

'Do you renounce Satan and all his works?' intoned the priest.

'Oh Father, don't ask me to answer that at a time like this. I'm going to a strange country and now is really not the time to make any enemies.'

I am in God's departure lounge and I've managed to miss quite a few scheduled flights.

– *Richard Harris*

'If the devil came across the two of us here now,' said the Englishman to the Irishman, 'who do you think he'd take away with him?'

'Me, of course,' responded the Irishman without a second's pause.

'Why's that?'

'Because he knows he can get you any time.'

Father Malachy was preaching a fiery sermon at the annual Redemptorist retreat.

'The end of the world is nigh,' he roared from the pulpit, 'and soon there will be a reckoning!' He cast his beady glare around the congregation. 'All those of you who want to go to heaven, stand up!' The entire congregation stood up.

'And all those of you who want to go to hell?'

Everyone remained seated. Then there was a shuffling sound from the third row as Little Seán stood up. You could have heard a pin drop. The priest did a double-take. This had never happened before during one of his sermons.

'You, there, do you want to go to hell?' he shouted, glaring at Little Seán.

'No, Father, to be sure and I don't. It doesn't sound like a nice class of place at all. But I felt sorry for you standing there all on your lonesome.'

Donal was 70 years old, had worked hard until he was 65 and had never taken a holiday or bought a new car for himself. His children were all married and he had been a widower for five years. He had saved all his life and as age crept up on him, he began to realise that he couldn't take any of it with him. So he decided to enjoy life for a change. He had a facelift, invested in hair implants, bought some expensive new suits and exchanged his old banger for a flashy red sports car. When he looked in the mirror, he saw a man at least ten years younger. One evening, he got all dressed up in his new clothes and sped off in his fancy car towards Dublin. Taking a bend too fast, he drove off the road into a huge tree and was killed instantly.

Arriving at the pearly gates, he decided to take St Peter to task.

'What's happened here?' he demanded furiously. 'I worked hard all my life, raised my family, was faithful to my wife – and just as I was starting to enjoy myself, I was killed stone dead. Why on earth did you allow that to happen?'

Saint Peter looked a bit embarrassed. He cleared his throat and said, 'Well, to tell you the honest truth, Donal, I just didn't recognise you.'

A rural water scheme was being rolled out across Ireland and hydrants for the emergency services were being placed at strategic points in built-up areas.

The director of the water board came to inspect the works and noticed that one of the hydrants had been placed beside the cemetery gates.

'What's that doing there? What possible use will it be beside a cemetery?' he asked one of the workers.

'You never know,' was the reply. 'Some of the fellas in there might be glad of a drop of cold water from time to time.'

Paddy was dying and he asked for a priest so he could make his last confession. As it was his last confession, he didn't want to tell any lies.

'The thing is, Father,' he said, 'my name's Paddy Murphy, but I haven't a bit of Irish blood in me.'

'Never mind,' said the priest. 'When you get to the pearly gates and St Peter comes out to greet you, just tell him your name and then keep your mouth shut.'

The Dear Departed

Bereavement is a time for grieving, but jokes in Ireland often reveal that the deceased might not always be greatly missed. Many of the jokes and stories that have to do with death focus on the fact that the bereaved spouse is not altogether unhappy, or that an insurance policy means that the deceased is certainly worth more dead than alive.

Nuala called in to the insurance office the day after her husband's funeral to collect the £10,000 that was owing to her on his life insurance policy. She looked at the cheque, wiped a tear from her eye and said, 'Oh dear me, I'd give a thousand pounds to have my poor Brian back with me.'

"And here's the good news..."

Joe saw Paddy digging his wife's grave and went over to commiserate.

'That'll do,' said Paddy, putting down his spade.

'But that hole can't be more than three foot deep!' said Joe. 'You can't bury her there. You'll have to dig down at least another three foot.'

'Ah well,' smiled Paddy, 'it'll do for her. I make it a rule in life never to make too much of a task out of pleasure.'

Séan knocked on his boss's door. 'I'd like a day off for my mother-in-law's funeral.'

'So would I, Séan, but she's a picture of health.'

Her grief lasted longer than I have ever known any woman's – three days.

– *Joseph Addison*

A woman moved out of a long bingo queue when a funeral passed by on the busy main street. She knelt down in the road, took out her rosary beads and started to pray.

'What are you doing, Mary?' hissed her friend, pulling her back into the queue. 'You'll lose us our places – we've been here ages and we're at the top of the line! We'll be inside in 10 minutes. Isn't it enough just to bless yourself?'

'Sure, why wouldn't I pray for him, Sheila?' replied Mary. 'Wasn't he a good husband to me all his life?'

Josie Dwyer had a reputation for being very tight with the money, but she was also one for keeping up appearances, so when her poor husband Brian died just after Christmas, she knew she'd need to buy a good suit to bury him in. Fortunately, the January sales had just started, so she was optimistic about finding a bargain.

Off she went into town, and came back two hours later laden with bags. Brian was laid out for the wake in his new suit, new shirt and new tie.

'Doesn't he look very well?' said Josie's good friend Sally when she came to give her condolences. 'Isn't that a fine suit he's wearing? I never saw it on him. Is it new?'

'It is, surely, and it was a great bargain in the sales,' said Josie. 'Didn't they throw in an extra pair of trousers for free!'

As Michael lay dying, he could hear the family gathered around him talking about the funeral.

'We'll get two funeral cars as well as the hearse,' whispered his wife.

'What do you need two cars for?' retorted her sister. 'Sure, isn't one more than enough?'

'The horse and cart would do just as well,' muttered his brother-in-law, under his breath.

Michael used every ounce of his strength to lift himself out of the bed. He started putting on his trousers.

'Come on, so,' he said. 'I'll walk to the cemetery now and save you the expense of the transport.'

———————

From a newspaper report about a botched
burglary that ended with a fatality:

'The murderer was clearly looking
for money, but luckily Mr Byrne
had put all his cash in the bank
earlier that day so the only thing
he lost in the burglary was his life.'

Joe, John and Mick were sitting at the bar one Friday night and the conversation turned to death and how they would like to be remembered.

'What would you like people to say at your funeral?' asked John.

'Well,' said Joe, 'when I die, the best thing they could say about me at my wake is that I was a great family man and my family never went short of anything.'

John disagreed. 'I'd like people to talk about all the good things I've achieved, all the ways I've given back to society.'

The men pondered this for while, nodding wisely over their pints.

'What about you, Mick? asked Joe. 'What would you like people to say at your wake?'

'That's easy,' said Mick. 'The one thing I'd really like them to say is, "Look, the corpse is breathing!"'

Brigid phoned the newspaper to dictate her husband's death notice. She was told that it would be a shilling a word. Brigid had only two shillings to spare, so she thought about it for a while and then she said, 'Just put "Joe died". Then everyone who knew him will know he's dead.' The woman in the newspaper office thought it was a bit stark for a death notice, so she offered Brigid three more words for nothing. Brigid thought again. 'Well,' she said, 'we could change it to "Joe died. Car going cheap."'

Wakes and Funerals

'May you never die until you see your own funeral' might seem a strange blessing, but at any wake or funeral you will hear it said more than once that the deceased would have enjoyed the great send-off they were getting. What a missed opportunity to see all your friends and relatives and hear your praises sung!

A family is never as close as when it's in mourning.

– Irish proverb

Q. What's the difference between an Irish wedding and an Irish wake?

A. One drunk fewer.

Funerals in Ireland are so jolly, they should be called funferalls.

– James Joyce

Given the unlikely options of attending a funeral or a sex orgy, a true Irishman will always opt for the funeral.

– John B. Keane

Waking the Dead

It's thought that the custom of waking the dead has its roots in the Celtic belief that death was the portal to a better life, so a funeral, despite the grief, was a good reason to celebrate. Traditionally, the wake was held in the deceased's house, and although in urban areas, the corpse is now often kept at a funeral home until it's brought to the church, the rural tradition remains to have the wake at home.

When someone dies, the window of the room is opened to release the soul, and then closed again two hours later to prevent it re-entering. Nobody is allowed to stand between the deceased and the window, as this might prevent the spirit leaving and is considered unlucky. All the clocks in the house are stopped at the time the person died. The mirrors are covered, at least in the room where the corpse is laid out, and the curtains are closed. The body is washed and dressed and placed in the coffin, which remains open throughout the wake; in days gone by many people belonged to a lay branch of one of the various religious orders, and they were dressed for burial in the habit of that order. Candles are lit at the head and foot of the coffin and are not extinguished until the coffin is removed to the church.

The wake is important both as a way to honour the deceased and as a way to help the bereaved to come to terms with their loss. Waking the dead is a long-standing Irish custom that has changed little over the centuries. A wake is not a solemn occasion – eating, drinking and storytelling are important aspects, all of which contribute to the cathartic nature of this unique way of saying farewell to a loved one. Old acquaintance is renewed – there's a saying that there are some people you only meet at funerals – and, as at any social gathering in Ireland, the craic can be mighty, particularly if the deceased has lived a long and happy life. Although it may seem somewhat paradoxical, wakes can be more enjoyable than many of the other gatherings we attend during our lives.

The best live entertainment in Ireland is a funeral.

– *Des MacHale*

'Wouldn't you like to die to have all those nice things said about you?'

– *Overheard after a funeral oration*

There are more lies told in a wake room than in a courtroom.

– *Irish proverb*

The Wake House

At a wake, friends and neighbours come to the house to view the body (there is usually an open coffin) and pay their respects to the bereaved family. Food and drink are offered (and cooked food is often brought by the mourners to the house) and the night is spent in prayer, reminiscence, tales and anecdotes about the deceased, always bearing in mind that it is frowned on to speak ill of the dead, no matter what faults they may have had.

Dead men tell no tales, but there's many a thing learned in a wake house.

– *Irish proverb*

Sign outside a Dublin undertakers:

'Buy your coffin now – guaranteed to last a lifetime'.

There's no point building a wall around a cemetery – those outside don't want to get in and those inside can't get out.

I am told he makes a very handsome corpse and becomes his coffin prodigiously.

– *Oliver Goldsmith*

Emer went to a neighbour's wake with her friend. She was viewing the body when her friend said, 'I never knew he was an atheist, did you?'

'I did not,' said Emer. 'And here he is, all dressed up and no place to go.'

The widow had her husband laid out for the wake, and he had the biggest smile on his face that was ever seen in Ireland. I said to her, 'I never saw a corpse with a smile like that. What happened to him?'

'Ah, dear God,' she said. 'The poor man. It was terrible. He was struck eight times by lightning and he thought he was having his photograph taken.'

– *Hal Roach*

Young Hugh died in a tractor accident on the farm. The weather was very warm, it being harvest time, so the wake lasted only one day, instead of the customary three. Despite that, a lot of drink was taken, because Hugh had been popular and everyone agreed it was a terrible shame for a fella to die so young.

When the time came to take the coffin to the church, one of the pallbearers was a little the worse for wear and he tripped as the coffin was being carried down the path. The coffin fell against the gatepost, and then the mourners heard a loud knocking coming from inside the coffin. Young Hugh wasn't dead at all!

The coffin was opened up, and everyone went back to the house to carry on with the party, this time celebrating Hugh's miraculous return from the dead. The next day, Hugh was in the middle of telling a joke when he keeled over and fell to the ground. This time he was really dead, stone dead.

So the wake started up again, and again the coffin was carried out of the house to the church.

'And for heaven's sake, Joe,' said the priest who was leading the mourners, 'don't drop the coffin again!'

Personally I have no bone to pick with graveyards.

– *Samuel Beckett*

___

An undertaker is the last man to let you down.

– *Jimmy O'Dea*

An undertaker and his friend walking down the main street stopped and removed their hats as a funeral went past.

'If the corpse was alive I'd have had that funeral,' the undertaker complained.

Blessings to See You on Your Way

Of course, it's not all jokes and laughter. As the night wears on, people come and go, songs are sung, and poetry is recited – increasing in sentimentality as the hours pass and more drink is taken. And what would an Irish wake be without a few blessings for the corpse?

May the good earth be soft under you when you rest upon it, and may it rest easy over you when at the last, you lay out under it, and may it rest so lightly over you that your soul may be out from under it quickly, and up, and off and on its way to God.

May every hair on your head turn into a candle to light your way to heaven, and may God and His Holy Mother take the harm of the years away from you.

———————

Dinny got blind drunk at his local pub in Ballycastle one Friday night and staggered home, taking his usual shortcut through the cemetery. He tripped into a newly dug grave, landed flat on his back and fell sound asleep.

The next morning, he was woken by the loud ringing of the church bells. He looked around him, saw all the headstones and said, 'Here we are, the Day of Judgment, and I'm the only one rising. It's a poor show for Ballycastle.'

You're a Long Time Dead

For many people, their burial place is of the utmost importance. And, when all is said and done, perhaps what's written on the grave can sum up a life better than anything else. Some of our greatest wit and humour (intentional or otherwise) can be found on the headstones that populate the graveyards scattered around Ireland. Sadly, with the increasing shortage of burial places and the move towards cremation rather than burial, epitaph writing may be a dying art.

My burying place is of no concern to me,
In the O'Connell circle let it be,
As to my funeral, all pomp is vain,
Illustrious people does prefer it plain.

– Zozimus

Epitaphs range from the intentionally funny:

Beneath this stone lies Murphy
They buried him today
He lived the life of Reilly
While Reilly was away

———————————

Beneath this stone lies Katherine my wife
In death my comfort, and my plague through life
Oh liberty! but soft I must not boast
She's haunt me else, by jingo, with her ghost

———————————

This stone was raised to Sarah Ford
Not Sarah's virtues to record –
For they're well known to all the town –
No, Lord: it was raised to keep her down.

I knew if I waited around long enough
Something like this would happen.

– Written as his own epitaph by George Bernard Shaw

To the simply punny:

Here lies the remains of
John Hall, Grocer
The world is not worth a fig.
I have good raisins for saying so.

To the hilariously badly arranged:

Erected to the memory of
JOHN PHILLIPS
Accidentally shot
As a mark of affection by his brother

In memory of
Richard Furlong
Who died 10th September 1859
Aged 23 years
This stone was erected by
Harry Alcock of Wilton Esq
Captain Wexford Regiment
In whose service he was killed by a
Horse falling on him
As a testimonial of respect and esteem.

Sir Robert Echlin, died 1757
Here lies a man without pretence,
Blessed with plain reason and common sense,
Calmly he looked on either life and here
Saw nothing to regret or there to fear.
From nature's temperate feast rose satisfied
Thanked Heaven that he lived, and that he died.

Sometimes an epitaph is a pious warning to those of us still living:

Stop!
Pray as you pass by
So as you are so once was I
As I am now so will you be
Prepare yourself and pray for me

Here lieth the remains
Of Richard Jones who
Departed this transitory life
On the 17th Day of
May 1809 in the 29th year of his age
When I was young and in my prime
It pleased the Lord to end my time
Like as the Lily fresh and green
I was cut down and no more seen
You old and young, see here I lie
As you are now so once was I.

All ye who roll in worldly bliss
Repent and follow me to this.

One of Ireland's most famous and frequently quoted
epitaphs is on the grave of W. B. Yeats, and comes from
one of his last poems, 'Under Ben Bulben':

Cast a cold Eye
On Life, on Death.
Horseman, pass by!

Brendan Behan 1923–1964

Shakespeare said pretty well everything and what he left out, James Joyce, with a nudge from meself, put in.

Brendan Francis Behan was born in Dublin on 9 February 1923 into a republican working-class family. The family lived in a house off Mountjoy Square that was one of several owned by his maternal grandmother. His father, a housepainter, was serving a prison term for republican activity when Behan was born. His maternal uncle was the composer of 'The Soldier's Song', the Irish national anthem, but it was from his father that Behan inherited his love of literature, Irish history and music. He went to school at St Vincent's in North William Street, moving on to the Christian Brothers School on the North Circular Road before apprenticing himself to his father at the age of 14 and signing up for a course at Bolton Street Technical School. He got some work as a housepainter, but he always had an ambition to be a writer.

Growing up in a republican household left its mark on Behan. He joined Fianna Éireann, the youth wing of the IRA, at the age of eight, moving on to membership of the parent organisation when he was just 16. On a trip to Liverpool in 1939, unsanctioned by the IRA, he was convicted of possession of explosives and spent the next three years in Borstal, after which he was deported to Dublin. In 1942 he was convicted of the attempted murder of two police detectives, intended to be carried out during a commemoration ceremony in Dublin for Wolfe Tone. Escaping

the death penalty, he was sentenced to 14 years' penal servitude, but was released in 1946 under a general amnesty for IRA prisoners. He left the IRA soon after his release.

Behan's work was first published in Fianna Éireann's magazine, *Fianna: The Voice of Young Ireland*, and he wrote his first play, *The Landlady*, while imprisoned in Mountjoy. He was published in the Irish literary journals of the day, including the highly regarded *The Bell*. In the 1950s he decided to go to Paris to make his name as a writer. He was soon getting his poetry published in periodicals and supporting himself as a journalist. He had also embarked on the heavy drinking that would be his downfall, to an extent that became unacceptable to his friends and acquaintances in Paris, and he returned to live in Ireland. In 1955 he married Beatrice Salkeld and they had one daughter, Blanaid, born in 1963.

His prison experiences provided material for his major literary works. His play *The Quare Fellow* (1954) was based on his time in Mountjoy, and his autobiography, *Borstal Boy* (1958), was an account of his first experience of incarceration. It was his last completed work and established his reputation as one of Ireland's leading writers. He started learning Irish while in Borstal, and when he was released, he went to the Galway Gaeltacht, where he stayed with a local family and became fluent. A considerable proportion of his literary output was in Irish – he wrote poetry and plays in that language; the original of his play *The Hostage* was *An Giall* (1958).

Behan had a larger-than-life personality, establishing a reputation early on in life as a hard drinker (his favourite drink was a strange mixture of champagne mixed with sherry), raconteur, entertainer and charmer – he was always the life and soul of the party. The quintessential Irishman, his assessment of his fellow countrymen was often both hilarious and extremely cutting, sometimes very close to the bone. His early reputation in London was helped along by a drunken television interview on BBC. He joked that he was 'a drinker with a writing problem'.

As the years progressed, he drank more and more heavily, becoming famous for his frequent drunken public appearances. He did more jail time for being drunk and disorderly. He was diagnosed with diabetes in 1956, although he had by then been diabetic for some years. Reason dictated that he should have curbed his drinking, but the medical advice he received seems to have had the opposite effect. Drink had contributed to his reputation, allowing his wit and talent to shine, but in later life it became his nemesis. He began to go into diabetic comas and have seizures, but would then discharge himself from hospital and immediately begin drinking again. What had once seemed charming and entertaining in him became less and less attractive to his public, who turned their backs on him, and publicans barred him from their pubs. Alcohol may have nurtured his muse in the early years, but he was now no longer able to produce his brilliant prose.

By 1964 his system had collapsed completely and he was hospitalised for the last time in March of that year. He died in the Meath Hospital on 20 March. His funeral is said to have been the biggest since the funeral of Charles Stewart Parnell and that of one of his own heroes, Michael Collins. An IRA guard of honour escorted the coffin to his final resting place in Glasnevin Cemetery.

There is a seated statue of Behan on a bench at Royal Canal Bank, between Drumcondra and Dorset Street, Dublin, and a bronze plaque outside the Palace Bar in Fleet Street, Dublin.

Quotes

Inspirations never go in for long engagements; they require immediate marriage to action.

A quotation in a speech, article or book is like a rifle in the hands of an infantryman. It speaks with authority.

Other people have a nationality. The Irish and the Jews have a psychosis.

If it was raining soup, the Irish would go out with forks.

One drink is too many for me and a thousand not enough.

It is a good deed to forget a poor joke.

The Irish are a very popular race – with themselves.

The big difference between sex for money and sex for free is that sex for money usually costs a lot less.

What an author likes to write most is his signature on the back of a cheque.

It's better to be criticised than ignored.

I took up writing because it's easier than house painting.

I only drink on two occasions – when I'm thirsty and when I'm not.

I respect kindness in human beings first of all, and kindness to animals. I don't respect the law; I have a total irreverence for anything connected with society except that which makes the roads safer, the beer stronger, the food cheaper and the old men and old women warmer in the winter and happier in the summer.

It's not that the Irish are cynical. It's simply that they have a wonderful lack of respect for everything and everybody.

Critics are like eunuchs in a harem; they know how it's done, they've seen it done every day, but they're unable to do it themselves.

If you greatly desire something, have the guts to stake everything on obtaining it.

If there were only three Irishmen left in the world you'd find two of them in a corner talking about the other. We're a backbiting race.

When I came back to Dublin I was courtmartialled in my absence and sentenced to death in my absence, so I said they could shoot me in my absence.

I saw a sign that said 'Drink Canada Dry'. So I did.

George Bernard Shaw 1856–1950

I often quote myself. It adds spice to my conversation.

One of Ireland's foremost dramatists, George Bernard Shaw was born in Synge Street in Dublin in 1856. His formal education was patchy – he hated school and had a lifelong antipathy towards the idea of schools, comparing them to prisons for the young (although he would later become a founder of the London School of Economics). Known as George by his family, he hated the name and preferred to be called Bernard.

Shaw was originally drawn to art rather than literature or drama. He studied at the Royal Dublin Society's drawing school and spent long hours in the National Gallery of Art on Merrion Square. He must have formed a considerable attachment to this institution, since he bequeathed it a third of his estate.

In 1872 Shaw's mother, Bessie, left his father and moved to London. Shaw followed her there in 1876 at the age of 19 – he would not return to Ireland for 30 years, and then only at the urging of his wife. As a Protestant in a predominantly Catholic country he belonged to the 'ascendancy', but his family was not prosperous and he was made feel inferior (or assumed feelings of inferiority) on many occasions in his youth. He grew a chip on his shoulder, which developed into something of a grudge against the country of his birth.

After his move to London, his mother supported him while he wrote novels, turning out five in five years, none of which was accepted for publication. Perhaps it was his mother who made him cynical about marriage and the position of women in society, a theme he would often explore in his literary works.

Shaw enjoyed the society of women, and had a long epistolary relationship with the actress Ellen Terry. On 1 June 1898 he married Charlotte Payne-Townshend, a wealthy woman who had provided a good chunk of the start-up capital for the London School of Economics. There was much speculation about the nature of their marriage, but it seems to have been happy, at least until Shaw became somewhat besotted with Mrs Patrick Campbell, an

actress in her late forties who was not a little miscast as the young Eliza Doolittle in Shaw's play *Pygmalion* in 1914. They seem to have embarked on an affair, but she had already decided to marry someone else and she abandoned the dress rehearsals of the play for her honeymoon. Despite everything that was going on in the background, *Pygmalion* was received to huge popular acclaim, but its run was suspended on the outbreak of war. Mrs Campbell then went with it to the US, where it was well received.

Shaw had a particular view of the world, with little time for the establishment of the day, declaring in the preface to his play *Man and Superman* that the 'art of government is the organisation of idolatry'. He was a founder member of the socialist Fabian society and was later a supporter of Stalin's communism. Through his activities with the Fabians, he was given some work as a music and theatre critic and this led to his becoming a playwright. After a not very noteworthy start – he found it difficult to find anyone willing to stage his plays, and his first production was a failure – he achieved huge success and notoriety. He was regarded in the profession as an actor's playwright – his stage directions were legendary, leaving absolutely no room for confusion. He was approached for film rights in his plays during the silent movie era in the 1920s, but he refused, knowing that producers were after his name rather than his work, which depended on the well-timed delivery of his razor-sharp dialogue. However, the advent of the 'talkies' opened up more possibilities. *Pygmalion* was filmed three times: in German, Dutch and English. It was a case of third time lucky. The famous play became a famous film, and the screenplay of *My Fair Lady* won an Oscar for Shaw in 1938.

Shaw's literary work became the vehicle for his sharp wit, which was soon generally referred to as 'Shavian'. However, his witticisms did not always spring from a desire to be amusing but were intended to make a point – political, moral or social.

A lifelong socialist, non-smoker, teetotaller and a convert to vegetarianism (he referred to his pre-vegetarian self as a 'cannibal'), he believed that communism was the fairest form of government, regarding democracy as a system that 'substitutes election by the incompetent many for appointment by the corrupt few'. His political views, frequently expressed in the long prefaces to his plays, were not always popular – espousing pacifism during the First World War was guaranteed not to win friends in Britain. He further damaged his popularity by taking the part of the 1916 Irish insurgents – almost a lone voice – although when their executions turned the tide of public opinion, he was on the right side in the end. He also campaigned against the execution of Roger Casement, a more popular, yet equally doomed cause.

Joan of Arc was canonised by the Catholic Church in 1920, and in 1923 Shaw began writing his great work, *Saint Joan*. This was his defining work, and it played worldwide. He was awarded the Nobel Prize in 1925 and joked that it must have been to celebrate the fact that he had written nothing that year. He quipped that 'Nobel Prize money is a lifebelt thrown to those who have already reached the shore safely'. He donated the prize money to the charitable endeavour of translating Swedish literary works into English. He refused all other honours and awards, including a knighthood.

Even in old age Shaw retained his interest in the issues of the time. In 1944 his book *Everybody's Political What's What* criticised the

failure of successive governments to distribute the national wealth fairly. He wrote it 'to track down some of the mistakes that have landed us in a gross misdistribution of domestic income and two world wars in twenty-five years'. He continued writing until his death in 1950, at the age of 94, the result of a fall from a tree that he was pruning in his garden at Ayot St Lawrence, Hertfordshire.

To date, he is the only person to have been honoured with both the Nobel Prize for Literature and an Oscar.

There is a statue of Shaw outside the National Gallery in Dublin and a plaque at his birthplace, 33 Synge Street, now the Shaw Museum, identifying him as the 'author of plays'.

Quotes

The only way for a woman to provide for herself decently is for her to be good to some man who can afford to be good to her.

Home is the girl's prison and the woman's workhouse.

A doctor's reputation is made by the number of eminent men who die under his care.

Dancing is a perpendicular expression of a horizontal desire.

I am enclosing two tickets to the first night of my new play; bring a friend ... if you have one.

– *George Bernard Shaw to Winston Churchill*

Cannot possibly attend first night; will attend second, if there is one.

– *Churchill's response*

Why should we take advice on sex from the pope? If he knows anything about it, he shouldn't!

You see things; you say, 'Why?' But I dream things that never were; and I say 'Why not?'

Animals are my friends …
and I don't eat my friends.

Patriotism is, fundamentally, a conviction that a particular country is the best in the world because you were born in it.

A drama critic is a man who leaves no turn unstoned.

She had lost the art of conversation, but not, unfortunately, the power of speech.

Those who cannot change their minds cannot change anything.

Certainly I enjoyed myself at your party. There was nothing else to enjoy.

The little I know, I owe to my ignorance.

Which painting in the National Gallery would I save if there was a fire? The one nearest the door, of course.

When a thing is funny, search it for a hidden truth.

I like flowers, I also like children, but I do not chop their heads off and keep them in bowls of water around the house.

Americans will go on adoring me until I say something nice about them.

The most tragic thing in the world is a man of genius who is not a man of honour.

James Joyce 1882–1941

Why don't you write books people can read?
– *Nora Barnacle Joyce*

James Augustine Aloysius Joyce was born in Rathgar, Dublin, on 2 February 1882, the eldest of ten surviving children born to John Stanislaus Joyce and Mary Jane 'May' Murray. His father was employed as a tax collector for Dublin Corporation from 1887 and the Joyce family moved to Bray, a fashionable seaside town in the neighbouring county of Wicklow. In 1891 John Joyce, as a result of a drinking habit and bad financial management, was declared bankrupt, and in 1893, was pensioned off by Dublin Corporation.

The family's financial problems had an effect on the education of the young Joyce. In 1888 he was enrolled in the prestigious Jesuit boarding school, Clongowes Wood College, but had to leave in 1892 when his father was no longer able to pay the fees. He was home-schooled for a while, and then at the O'Connell School run by the Christian Brothers at North Richmond Street in Dublin. In 1893 a Jesuit acquaintance of the family arranged for him to be awarded a partial bursary so that he could attend another Jesuit institution, Belvedere College in Dublin, a day school.

After leaving school, Joyce attended the newly established University College Dublin, reading English, French and Italian. He was involved in Dublin theatrical and literary circles, writing articles and plays. In 1900 his first piece of work, a review of Ibsen's *When We Dead Awaken*, was published in the *Fortnightly Review*.

Joyce graduated from UCD with a BA in 1902 and decided to go to Paris to study medicine – he soon dropped out, pleading illness and the difficulty of dealing with the cold weather as reasons. He remained in Paris until his mother was diagnosed with cancer, when he returned to Dublin. After her death, he stayed on in Dublin and began to drink quite heavily. The family's financial situation was parlous, and he wrote book reviews, taught and sang for a living – he had a good voice, and won a bronze medal in the Tenor Competition at the 1904 Feis Ceoil.

1904 was also the year he met Nora Barnacle, a young woman from Galway who was working as a chambermaid in Finn's Hotel in Dublin. They had their first date on 16 June, a day that is now

immortalised as Bloomsday, the day on which all the action in Joyce's novel *Ulysses* takes place. Later that year the couple left for the Continent, ending up in Trieste, where he taught in the Berlitz School for almost 10 years.

In 1905 James and Nora's first child, Giorgio, was born. Joyce moved to Rome in 1906 to work as a clerk in a bank, but moved back to Trieste in 1907, the year that his daughter Lucia was born. In 1909 he came to Dublin to launch Ireland's first cinema, the Volta Cinematograph, which was backed by some businessmen in Trieste, and it was very successful until Joyce returned to Trieste in 1910. He came back to Dublin for the last time in his life in 1912, in a final, unsuccessful, attempt to have *Dubliners*, his collection of short stories, published.

By now, the eye problems that would bedevil Joyce throughout the rest of his life had manifested themselves. Financially, he was scraping by on teaching and loans. In 1915 he moved to Zurich and it was here that he met the philanthropist Harriet Shaw Weaver. She funded his writing for the next 25 years, enabling him to give up teaching. While in Zurich he started work on *Ulysses*.

He went back to Trieste after the war, and accepted an invitation to Paris from Ezra Pound, intending to stay for a week. He remained there for the next 20 years. His reputation as an avant-garde writer became established during his years in Paris, where he continued to be funded by Shaw Weaver.

Joyce's defining work, the novel *Ulysses*, was first published in serial form in the magazine *The Little Review*, beginning in 1918, but in 1920 the serialisation was halted as the result of a finding of obscenity by the US courts. The novel wasn't published in the US until 1933, and Joyce had problems finding a publisher this side of the pond, until Sylvia Beach, owner of the Paris bookshop Shakespeare and Company, undertook publication of a limited print-run in 1922. *Ulysses* is famous for its 'stream of consciousness' narrative style, and for its very detailed depiction of the city of Dublin. Joyce set it on 16 June 1904 and he used the 1904 edition of *Thom's Street Directory* to ensure accuracy.

In 1923, after a short break to recover his energies, Joyce started work on *Finnegans Wake*, pushing the techniques used in *Ulysses* to their limit. In 1931 his father died, and with his daughter's mental health problems (she had been diagnosed schizophrenic) and his own failing eyesight, his work rate slowed. The book was eventually published in 1939. The following year, the Nazi occupation of Paris impelled him to return to Zurich.

On 11 January 1941 Joyce had surgery for a perforated ulcer in a hospital in Zurich. He recovered from the operation but had a relapse the next day and went into a coma. He died on 13 January and he was buried in Fluntern cemetery.

Nora Barnacle Joyce's offer to the Irish government to have his remains transferred to Dublin was not accepted, probably because of his anti-Catholic stance. The *Irish Independent* commented later that year: '[James Joyce] died in Zurich early this year, having … reviled the religion in which he had been brought up and fouled the nest which was his native city.'

However, since then, Joyce has been honoured by his native city with numerous wall plaques, including one at his birthplace in Brighton Square, Rathgar, a bust in St Stephen's Green and a statue in North Earl Street, irreverently referred to by Dubliners as 'the prick with the stick'. The 14 bronze pavement plaques of the Ulysses Walk in Dublin commemorate the route taken by Leopold Bloom in the novel. In 2003 the James Joyce Bridge, spanning the River Liffey in Dublin city, was opened. In April 2013 the Central Bank issued a silver €10 coin in his honour that misquoted a line from *Ulysses* (although 10,000 were minted and sold), and the Irish Navy's offshore patrol vessel, the LÉ *James Joyce*, was launched in 1915.

Quotes

God made food;
the devil the cooks.

Can't bring back time. Like
holding water in your hand.

Shakespeare is the happy
hunting ground of all
minds that have lost
their balance.

Every jackass going the
roads thinks he has ideas.

Mistakes are the portals
of discovery.

A man of genius makes
no mistakes. His errors
are volitional and are the
portals of discovery.

What's yours is mine and
what's mine is my own.

Think you're escaping and
run into yourself. Longest
way round is the shortest
way home.

Life is too short to
read a bad book.

In the particular is contained the universal.

I care not if I live but a day and a night, so long as my deeds live after me.

Good puzzle would be cross Dublin without passing a pub.

When I die, Dublin will be written on my heart.

He is cured by faith who is sick of fate.

Reproduction is the beginning of death.

Your mind will give back exactly what you put into it.

Beware the horns of a bull, the heels of the horse, and the smile of an Englishman.

History ... is a nightmare from which I am trying to wake.

Jonathan Swift 1667–1745

... He gave the little wealth he had,
To build a house for fools and mad ...

Jonathan Swift – clergyman, poet, essayist, satirist – is one of Ireland's best-known wits, with probably more witticisms attributed to him than he wrote or uttered during his lifetime. Maurice Craig said that he 'has been the occasion of more nonsense than any other writer except Shakespeare'.

He was famous even in his own time, and he was one of those great writers who 'so affected popular imagination in their lifetime that a ghost of them survives, vaguely familiar to thousands who in reality know nothing but the name'. (Stephen Gwynne)

This 'ghost' is the Swift who has lived on in the public imagination, but he was a man of many parts.

Swift was born in Dublin on 3 November 1687. His father died when he was very young and he never really knew his mother. To all intents and purposes he was an orphan, taken under the wing of

a wealthy uncle, Godwin Swift, who saw to it that the boy received a good education at the Kilkenny Grammar School (believed to have been the best school in Ireland at that time). He then went up to Trinity College Dublin, at that time just a simple, brick-built quadrangle, graduating with a bachelor's degree at the age of 18. He had just embarked on further study for a master's degree when political unrest in Ireland plunged Trinity into chaos, with most of the dons fleeing Ireland. Swift decided that it would also be expedient for him to leave and he went to England.

The same uncle found him a position as secretary and assistant to Sir William Temple in Farnham, Surrey, and it was there that he met the eight-year-old Esther Johnson, a ward in Sir William's care. Swift became her tutor, and she became the 'Stella' who occupied so much of his thoughts.

Swift became ill in 1692, left Sir William's service and went back to Ireland. In 1693 he took holy orders in the Church of Ireland and was appointed to a remote community in Antrim, which was not to his liking. In 1696 he returned to Temple's service, until 1699, when Sir William died. Swift, usually quick with the barbed epigram, said that 'all that was good and amiable in humankind' had died with him. High praise, indeed, from the man who would become renowned for his savage wit.

Always hopeful of advancement in his chosen profession, the Church, Swift accepted a living in Ireland that had a connection to St Patrick's Cathedral in Dublin. He travelled frequently between Dublin and London; when he returned to Dublin from one of his trips, he brought with him the 20-year-old Stella, who was his muse and companion for the rest of her life. Rumours that they were married abounded, but these were always denied by those who knew Stella well. The rumours are likely to be untrue – what reason would they have had for keeping their marriage secret?

Swift began to gain a reputation as a writer and his first major work, *A Tale of a Tub*, was a masterly satire on religion, regarded by many, including Queen Anne, at the time of its publication as deeply profane. In a period when Church and State were intertwined, the book could be regarded as having been an ill-timed move by an ambitious young clergyman.

Swift was also becoming more politically active, allying himself with the Tory cause. He hoped to be given a good Church appointment in England, but he had backed the wrong horse. The Whigs came to power and the young clergyman's ambitions were thwarted. Friends lobbied on his behalf and he was eventually awarded the deanery of St Patrick's Cathedral, a position he held until his death. For someone with ambitions to the episcopacy, this must have seemed like a dead end.

Returning to Dublin to take up his new appointment, a move that he saw as dooming him to die 'in a rage, like a poisoned rat in a hole', Swift's innate sense of humanity and justice soon moved him to take the part of the Irish people against British government policies. He threw himself into pamphleteering, achieving major success and a reputation as a patriot with his works supporting Irish causes, through the medium of biting satire. His pamphlets included *A Modest Proposal*, which highlighted the poverty of the Irish people, and *The Drapier's Letters*, which was an attempt to undermine the government's ambitions to flood Ireland with debased coin in order to turn a profit. *A Modest Proposal* was a particularly difficult read, and remains so today, recommending as a cure for the poverty endemic in the country that the children

of the poor be used to feed the rich – Swift describes the best way of cooking them, offering the unpalatable advice that a child 'will make two dishes as an entertainment for friends'. His most famous and enduring work, however, is the novel *Gulliver's Travels*, which was an immediate success when it was published in 1726. A satire on the times in which he lived, every voyage in the book (there are four) is an instruction on the dangers of succumbing to the sin of pride, or hubris. It is now regarded as an attack on Enlightenment thinking, in which Swift found many shortcomings.

In his personal life Swift cultivated the friendship of men of letters, including Alexander Pope, and he also became involved with a young woman called Hester Vanhomrigh, who followed him from London to Dublin. Swift called her 'Vanessa', and he kept his relationship with her a secret from Stella. Vanessa died in 1723 and Stella died in 1728, this latter death a devastating blow for Swift. His letters to her were published posthumously in 1766 as *The Journal to Stella*.

After Stella's death, Swift's health, always problematic, became increasingly compromised – it is thought that he may have suffered throughout his adult life from the debilitating, and at the time undiscovered, Menière's disease. His memory and his hearing deteriorated and he began to lose his mind. Always irascible, his temper became more unpredictable and, increasingly, he alienated his friends.

In 1742 he had a stroke and was declared as being of unsound mind, although this may have been a device utilised by his friends to distance the hangers-on with which he was surrounded. He lived on in St Patrick's deanery, increasingly unable to care for himself, to read or to write – a mere shell of the vital man he had once been.

Despite his literary success and the recognition he received during his lifetime, Swift displayed the hallmarks of disappointment throughout his adult life – being thwarted in his clerical ambitions may have given rise to the scathing satire that became his trademark.

He died on 19 October 1745 and was buried in his cathedral. He willed his modest fortune for the foundation of a hospital for the insane in Dublin. Today, St Patrick's Hospital is Ireland's largest independent mental health service.

Swift wrote his own epitaph, in Latin, which is attached to the wall on the south aisle of the cathedral. It was poetically translated by W. B. Yeats:

> Swift has sailed into his rest
> Savage indignation there
> Cannot lacerate his breast.
> Imitate him if you dare,
> World-besotted traveller; he
> Served human liberty

There is a plaque commemorating Swift's birthplace at Little Ship Street near Dublin Castle.

Quotes

Every man desires to live long, but no man wishes to be old.

Blessed is he who expects nothing, for he shall never be disappointed.

The power of fortune is confessed only by the miserable, for the happy impute all their success to prudence or merit.

He was a bold man that first ate an oyster.

Vision is the art of seeing what is invisible to others.

Power is no blessing in itself, except when it is used to protect the innocent.

I never wonder to see men wicked, but I often wonder to see them not ashamed.

A tavern is a place where madness is sold by the bottle.

The proper words in the proper places are the true definition of style.

Observation is an old man's memory.

The stoical scheme of supplying our wants by lopping off our desires, is like cutting off our feet when we want shoes.

Nothing is so great an example of bad manners as flattery. If you flatter all the company, you please none; If you flatter only one or two, you offend the rest.

Don't set your wit against a child.

One enemy can do more hurt than ten friends can do good.

Books, the children of the brain.

Argument is the worst sort of conversation.

Every dog must have his day.

Invention is the talent of youth, as judgement is of age.

Promises and pie-crusts are made to be broken.

There is nothing constant in this world but inconsistency.

When a true genius appears in this world, you may know him by this sign, that the dunces are all in confederacy against him.

In Church your grandsire cut his throat;
To do the job too long he tarried.
He should have had my hearty vote,
To cut his throat before he married.

Lady Augusta Gregory 1852–1932

What makes Ireland inclined toward the drama is that it's a great country for conversation.

Isabella Augusta Persse was born in County Galway on 15 March 1852, to a landed Anglo-Irish family with a large estate at Roxborough (like so many 'big houses', Roxborough House was burnt down during the Irish Civil War). In common with all female children of her class she was educated at home and her Irish-speaking nanny sparked a lifelong interest in Irish history, language and folklore. Lady Gregory is now remembered as a driving force behind the Irish Literary Revival of the late 19th and early 20th centuries and the founding of a national theatre.

In 1880 she married a former Governor of Ceylon, Sir William Gregory, and was known thereafter as Lady Gregory. A widower 35 years her senior, Sir William had an estate, Coole Park, at Gort, County Galway, later made famous in the poetry of W. B. Yeats. He had wide-ranging interests in the arts and literature and the couple spent a lot of time at his house in London. They held a

weekly literary salon there, attended by such luminaries as Robert Browning, Henry James and Alfred Lord Tennyson. They had one child, Robert, who was killed in action as an airman in the First World War.

The couple travelled widely – in India, Egypt, Spain and Italy. Soon after her marriage Lady Gregory began to write pamphlets, stories and poems, although much of her writing was never published. When Sir William died in 1892, she returned to Coole Park to edit his memoir.

A visit to the Aran Islands the following year rekindled her interest in all things Irish and she began collecting myths and legends for publication. In the meantime, her work on her husband's memoir was so well received that she decided to edit his grandfather's correspondence. Work on this gave her such an insight into Irish history that she developed 'a dislike and distrust of England' and aligned her position with Irish nationalism and republicanism.

In 1896 Lady Gregory met the poet W. B. Yeats on a visit to Edward Martyn. Yeats described her as 'a plainly dressed woman of forty-five, without obvious good looks, except the charm that

NO. 2. SECOND YEAR.

A BROADSIDE

FOR JULY, 1909.
PUBLISHED MONTHLY BY E. C. YEATS AT THE CUALA PRESS,
CHURCHTOWN, DUNDRUM, COUNTY DUBLIN.
SUBSCRIPTION TWELVE SHILLINGS A YEAR POST FREE.

A WARNING
Translated by Lady Gregory from the Irish
of An Chrasibhin

You will go, you will see, and you will love,
  Believe me;
You will turn back to her when you go away,
  That is it !
You will come, you will follow, and you will begin
  Soft talk;
You will be whispering with her till you kiss
  Her hand;
You will be whispering with her till you kiss
  Her mouth;
And when that way you have got into her net
  You will marry herself.
After that, you will be doing repentance
  Every day.
It is I that tell it to you, and you will be bound
  For ever!

300 copies only.

comes from strength, intelligence and kindness'. The trio became interested in the idea of an Irish theatre and the Irish Literary Theatre was founded in 1899. In 1901 the theatre, always short of funds, folded. However, the desire for a national theatre had taken root, and in 1904 Gregory collaborated with Yeats, Martyn, J. M. Synge, George Russell, Annie Horniman and William and Frank Fay to found the Irish National Theatre Society, ultimately buying the site of the Hibernian Theatre of Varieties in Lower Abbey Street in Dublin.

Lady Gregory's play *Spreading the News* was performed on the opening night at the new premises, 27 December 1904. She was active as a director of the Abbey Theatre until her retirement in 1928 because of ill health. With a reputation for austerity in her private life, she had worked tirelessly for the promotion of the theatre and on translations of Irish folk tales. George Moore once joked that 'If I were to write *Diarmuid and Gráinne* in French, Lady Gregory would then translate my French into English; O'Donoghue would then translate the English into Irish, and then Lady Gregory would translate the Irish into English. After that, Yeats would put style on it.'

She had a great talent as a peace-broker in the many disputes between the larger-than-life personalities who were her co-founders of the Abbey Theatre. She wrote or translated almost 40 plays, mostly gentle folk comedies. These were popular with early audiences, providing lighter interludes in the diet of tragic drama produced by the literary heavyweights of the day. Nowadays her plays seem very dated and are rarely performed.

After she retired, she continued to keep literary open house at Coole Park, which by then had been sold to the Irish Forestry Commission, although she had retained the right to live there during her life. The house was demolished in 1941, but the park itself is now a nature reserve. One of the trees in the park is an informal record of our literary and artistic heritage, bearing the carved initials of J. M. Synge, George Russell (Æ), George Bernard Shaw, W. B. Yeats, Jack Yeats, George Moore, Katharine Tynan, Violet Martin and Sean O'Casey.

Lady Gregory died of breast cancer on 22 May 1932. Apart from the plays she wrote and translated, she had written prolifically during her lifetime, producing long narrative accounts based on the Irish myths and legends, published as *Cuchulain of Muirthemne* in 1902, with a later volume, *Gods and Fighting Men,* appearing in 1904. The dialogue in her stories is in an invented transliteration of Irish known as Kiltartanese, named after the nearby village of Kiltartan. She also wrote a comprehensive study of local folklore, published in 1920 as *Visions and Beliefs in the West of Ireland*. Throughout her adult life she kept detailed diaries and journals, which give an insight into life and literature in Ireland in the first 30 years of the 20th century. According to George Bernard Shaw, she was 'the greatest living Irishwoman'.

The Kiltartan Gregory Museum, built as a school by Sir William Gregory, houses a collection of memorabilia and manuscripts relating to the Gregory family and the Irish literary renaissance, to which Lady Gregory made such a huge contribution.

Quotes

It is not always them that has the most that makes the most show.

I'll take no charity! What I get I'll earn by taking it. I would feel no pleasure in it being given to me, any more than a huntsman would take pleasure being made a present of a dead fox, in place of getting a run across country after it.

People put more in their prayers than was ever put in them by God.

It takes madness to find out madness.

It is the old battle, between those who use a toothbrush and those who don't.

Curses on them that boil eggs too hard! What use is an egg that is hard to any person on earth?

Every day in the year there comes some malice into the world, and where it comes from is no good place.

I feel more and more the time wasted that is not spent in Ireland.

It's best make changes little by little, the same as you'd put clothes upon a growing child.

There is no sin coveting things that are of no great use or profit, but would show out good and have some grandeur around them.

Every trick is an old one, but with a change of players, a change of dress, it comes out as new as before.

The way most people fail is in not keeping up the heart.

Oliver Goldsmith 1728–1774

Success consists of getting up just one more time than you fall.

Oliver Goldsmith, son of a Church of Ireland clergyman, was born in Longford. The actual date of his birth is uncertain, although he is supposed to have told a biographer that it was 10 November 1728. His family is thought to have lived in genteel poverty, but when Goldsmith was two they moved to a large parsonage at Lissoy, near Athlone, County Westmeath, when his father was made rector of the parish there. The boy went to school at an academy in Elphin run by his grandfather, and then up to Trinity College Dublin to study theology and law. As a student, he was a typically poor one, missing lectures, drinking, gambling and generally having a good time. He graduated in 1749 at the bottom of his class, sufficiently badly that neither the church nor the legal profession would accept him into their ranks. His relatives decided to fund his study of medicine at Edinburgh from 1752 to 1755, and he subsequently used the title 'Doctor', even though he went down without a degree.

Probably the original drop-out, Goldsmith then undertook the Grand Tour – on foot – through the Low Countries, France, Switzerland and Northern Italy, supporting himself by busking with his flute. Returning to London in 1756, he worked at a variety of jobs – apothecary's assistant, school usher, physician (although his patients were usually too poor to pay him), writer and translator. He wrote articles and essays for many of London's periodicals and several huge and inaccurate histories; he is also said to have been willing to translate just about anything. He started working for the *Monthly Review*, the first publication to provide literary and other criticism. He was also writing for himself; his satirical essay 'Citizen of the World' established his reputation as an essayist in an era when the essay was a common literary form. Goldsmith was soon on social terms with the literary greats of the day, including Samuel Johnson, James Boswell, Joshua Reynolds, Edmund Burke and David Garrick. By 1764, the year in which his long poem 'The Traveller' was published, he had become one of the founding members of 'The Club', a literary club that met weekly.

Unprepossessing, even ugly, in appearance, disorganised, socially gauche with poor conversation skills and, in an era of great orators, displaying absolutely no talent for public speaking, Goldsmith had one great advantage – he was a wonderful writer, a fact acknowledged by his peers and still recognised today. His lightness of touch has an appeal for everyone. David Garrick once wrote a cod epigraph for him:

> Here lies Nolly Goldsmith, for shortness called Noll,
> Who wrote like an angel, but talked like poor Poll.

Samuel Johnson summarised him somewhat less flippantly: 'No man was more foolish when he had not a pen in his hand, or more wise when he had.'

Given the accolades, the works for which he is remembered are few – two long poems, 'The Traveller' and 'The Deserted Village', a novel, *The Vicar of Wakefield*, and two plays, *The Good-Natur'd Man* and *She Stoops to Conquer*. *The Vicar of Wakefield* is still immensely popular – beautifully crafted, with a most unlikely, yet likeable hero, Dr Primrose, the novel was, long before Dickens, a vehicle for subtle social comment. Drawing on his own family's experience, he invented well-rounded characters to whom the reader can relate.

That the novel's popularity has endured for 250 years is a clear indication of the genius of the author.

She Stoops to Conquer, a delightful farce, was an immediate hit, even though its producer believed that it was doomed to failure. It is a play that wears its age lightly, and it is still performed all over the English-speaking world.

'The Deserted Village' was another vehicle for some topical social comment – the Enclosures Acts of the 17th century allowed landowners to remove all their land from common use, resulting in mass depopulation of the countryside. Goldsmith's long poem is an unveiled critique of the immorality of this development:

> The man of wealth and pride
> Takes up a space that many poor supplied;
> Space for his lake, his park's extended bounds,
> Space for his horses, equipage, and hounds:
> The robe that wraps his limbs in silken sloth
> Has robbed the neighbouring fields of half their growth.

Goldsmith himself was perennially short of money, and he knew what misery was caused by its lack. However, unlike many of his contemporaries, he believed that wealth was not the key to happiness, and he deplored the excessive wealth of the few in 18th-century Britain.

Goldsmith seems to have retained his spirit of adventure throughout his life, professing a desire to go to India and set himself up as a surgeon there. Even at the height of his literary success, he still kept that hope alive. It never happened, and another, more advanced plan to travel to America was thwarted when he missed the boat that would have taken him there. He had a great zest for life and seems always to have wanted more – more adulation, more popularity and, simply, to be better. It could never

have been said of him that he was a man of no ambition.

In 1774, Goldsmith became ill – he diagnosed himself (perhaps wrongly) with a kidney infection, his condition worsened and he died after a short illness, leaving nothing but debts and his wonderful literary legacy. He was buried in Temple Church in London. There is an epitaph by Samuel Johnson in Westminster Abbey. Translated from the original Latin, it reads:

> Oliver Goldsmith: A Poet, Naturalist, and Historian,
> who left scarcely any style of writing untouched,
> and touched nothing that he did not adorn.
> Of all the passions, whether smiles were to move or tears,
> a powerful yet gentle master.
> In genius, vivid, versatile, sublime.
> In style, clear, elevated, elegant.

There is a monument to Goldsmith in the centre of Ballymahon. Despite his undistinguished career at Trinity College Dublin, a statue of him was erected there in the 19th century and one of the newer lecture theatres there has been named in his honour.

Quotes

People seldom improve when they have no model other than themselves to copy.

The wise are polite all the world over – but fools are polite only at home.

Hope is such a bait, it covers any hook.

Write how you want, the critic shall show the world you could have written better.

I love every thing that is old; old friends, old times, old manners, old books, old wines.

As writers become more numerous, it is natural for readers to become more indolent; whence must necessarily arise a desire of attaining knowledge with the greatest possible ease.

Ceremonies are different in every country, but true politeness is everywhere the same.

Pity and friendship are two passions incompatible with each other.

Ask me no questions and I'll tell you no fibs.

Every absurdity has a champion to defend it.

Don't let us make imaginary evils, when you know we have so many real ones to counter.

They say women and music should never be dated.

To a philosopher no circumstance, however trifling, is too minute.

He who fights and runs away may live to fight another day.

As ten millions of circles can never make a square, so the united voice of myriads cannot lend the smallest foundation to falsehood.

The virtue which requires to be ever guarded is scarcely worth the sentinel.

Oscar Wilde 1854–1900

I have nothing to declare except my genius.

Poet, playwright, critic and aesthete, Oscar Fingal O'Flahertie Wills Wilde was born in Dublin on 16 October 1854. His father, Sir William Wilde, was a highly regarded and philanthropic doctor specialising in diseases of the eye. His mother, Lady Jane 'Speranza' Wilde, was a poet who hosted a renowned literary salon. Wilde was a clever boy – he was sent to school at the Portora Royal School in Enniskillen and had a particular interest in classics. He was awarded a classics scholarship at Trinity College Dublin, where he excelled himself, receiving a further scholarship to Magdalen College, Oxford. His academic star continued to rise and he graduated with a first in classics.

While at Oxford he had embarked on the creative writing for which he would become so famous. On coming down from Oxford he moved to London, where he continued to write. His first publication, in 1881, was a collection of poetry, aptly titled *Poems*.

Although Wilde is now best-known for his witticisms, epigrams and throwaway remarks, he began his career, as he meant to proceed, as a serious writer. *Poems* established his reputation and he was offered a nine-month lecture tour in the US, a great coup for such a young writer. While on tour, he met two of his literary heroes, Henry Wadsworth Longfellow and Walt Whitman, and his admiration for them was mirrored by theirs for him.

Leaving the US after his highly successful tour, he immediately embarked on a second lecture tour of Ireland and England. It was at this time that Wilde set himself up as a leader of the aesthetic movement, which pursued beauty for its own sake – this may have given rise to his lasting reputation as a louche effete.

His lecture tour ended in 1884, and he married Constance Lloyd on 29 May of that year. His sons Cyril and Vyvyan were born within two years. In 1885 Wilde was given the editorship of a failing women's magazine, *Lady's World*, in an attempt to increase its circulation. Re-titling it *Women's World*, he broadened its scope from beauty and fashion to provide a forum for women's opinions on a range of subjects, including art and literature.

In 1888, Wilde published his second book, this time a highly successful collection of moving and multi-layered children's stories – *The Happy Prince and Other Tales*. In 1891 his only novel, *The Picture of Dorian Gray*, was published. This time, there was little critical acclaim, opinion at the time considering that the book was immoral in its portrayal of a beautiful young man whose life of pleasure and sin is unreflected in his ageless appearance, while his painted portrait changes constantly to show the effects of advancing age and his debauched lifestyle.

In 1892 the first of Wilde's four comedies mocking the mores and restrictions of Victorian life were performed on the London stage, to enormous popular and critical acclaim. *Lady Windermere's Fan* was so successful that Wilde began to devote himself almost exclusively to writing plays. It was followed by *A Woman of No Importance* (1893), *An Ideal Husband* (1895) and *The Importance of Being Earnest* (1895). Immensely popular in their day, the plays are still performed and still resonate with contemporary audiences. Wilde could be savage in his wit, as is demonstrated in his reaction to the players who had just performed *The Importance of Being Earnest*:

My dear delightful company, I have just watched your performance of *The Importance of Being Earnest*. It reminded me of a play I once wrote.

Wilde was now at the height of his fame, riding a wave of success, making a lot of money and being fêted by London society. It was at this time also that he struck up a relationship with Lord Alfred Douglas, a young man known affectionately to Wilde as 'Bosie'. Wilde's homosexuality was no secret, but it was largely tolerated, the law seemingly turning a blind eye to his tendencies. However, Douglas's father, the Marquess of Queensberry, was outraged by his son's liaison. He took issue with Wilde, accusing him in a mis-spelled note of being a sodomite. Wilde made the worst decision of his life, one that caused everything to unravel, when he sued Queensberry for criminal libel. In effect he demolished his own case by obeying what must have been an irresistible impulse to allow his wit to sparkle. His flippant responses to defence counsel during the trial provoked much laughter in the courtroom, but led him, as the defence intended, along a path to the point where evidence of his homosexuality could be produced. His libel suit was dismissed and the spotlight of the law was turned on him. Arrested on charges of gross indecency, in May 1895 he was convicted and sentenced to two years' hard labour. Handing down the maximum sentence, the judge said it was 'the worst case' he had ever heard and expressed the wish that the sentence could have been greater. The hardship and privations of prison destroyed Wilde's health and spirit. When he was released in 1897 he went to Paris, never to return to England or Ireland. His poem 'The Ballad of Reading Gaol' (1898), his only major work subsequent to his incarceration is, in effect, his prison diary.

In the immediate aftermath of Wilde's conviction, Constance Wilde, who had turned a blind eye to his lifestyle, changed her surname and that of their children to Holland, in an attempt to distance them from the scandal of the case. She made Wilde give up his parental rights, although they never divorced. She died in 1898, predeceasing her husband by two years.

His money gone, Wilde lived in Paris for the remainder of his life, staying in cheap hotels and the apartments of friends. In November 1900 he had an operation on his ear for a condition resulting from an injury suffered during his time in prison; it wasn't successful and he died of cerebral meningitis on 30 November 1900. His remains were eventually moved to the famous Parisian cemetery Père Lachaise, his tomb guarded by a modernistic angel carved by the sculptor Jacob Epstein.

His epitaph, from 'The Ballad of Reading Gaol', reads:

> And alien tears will fill for him
> Pity's long-broken urn,
> For his mourners will be outcast men,
> And outcasts always mourn

It was unlikely that anyone of Wilde's talent and wit would be forgotten and his name and reputation live on in his many witticisms and *bons mots*. He was celebrated as a wit and dramatist in the decades following his death, and had become a university subject by the 1960s. His witty aphorisms, his stories and plays have an eternal freshness and he continues to be quoted (and misquoted).

In 1997 a statue of Wilde was placed in Merrion Square, Dublin, opposite his boyhood home, which bears a plaque in his honour.

Quotes

Consistency is the last refuge of the unimaginative.

I can resist everything except temptation.

The play was a great success but the audience was a disaster.

No good deed ever goes unpunished.

The English country gentleman galloping after a fox – the unspeakable in pursuit of the uneatable.

Punctuality is the thief of time.

It is very easy to endure the difficulties of one's enemies – it is the successes of one's friends that are hard to bear.

It is a very sad thing that nowadays there is so little useless information around.

When the gods want to punish us they answer our prayers.

I sometimes think that God in creating man somewhat overestimated His ability.

A cynic is a man who knows the price of everything and the value of nothing.

The truth is rarely pure, and never simple.

A little sincerity is a dangerous thing and a great deal of it is absolutely fatal.

When you convert someone to an idea you lose faith in it.

Duty is what one expects from others. It is not what one does oneself.

Morality is simply the attitude we adopt towards people whom we personally dislike.

Questions are never indiscreet. Answers sometimes are.

There is only one thing worse than being talked about and that is not being talked about.

I hear her hair has turned quite gold from grief.

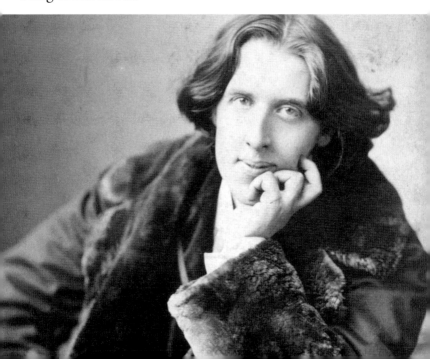

Samuel Beckett 1906-1989

When are they going to stop making me mean more than I say?

Samuel Barclay Beckett was born in Dublin on 13 April 1906. His family was Anglican and they lived in the Dublin suburb of Foxrock. After he finished preparatory school, Beckett attended the Portora Royal School in Enniskillen as a boarder. He was not very outgoing, but excelled academically and was a keen sportsman. In 1923 he started an arts degree at Trinity College Dublin and represented the college in various sports. In 1926 he won a college scholarship and graduated as a gold medallist in his finals in 1927. After graduation he was offered an exchange lectureship at the École Normale Supérieure in Paris, but it was postponed, so he taught French at Campbell College in Belfast for two terms while waiting to take up the post.

In 1928 he moved to Paris and began teaching at the École Normale. He was befriended by James Joyce who was very encouraging about his writing, although a liaison between Beckett and Joyce's daughter, Lucia, cooled the friendship for a time. Encouraged by Joyce, Beckett began to put his work forward for publication – first a story, then some poems and a long essay. He returned to Dublin in 1930 to teach French at TCD. A talented musician, he was also interested and active in drama, and was not convinced that he was cut out to be either a teacher or a writer. He resigned from TCD in 1931 and went back to Paris.

SAMVEL BECKETT

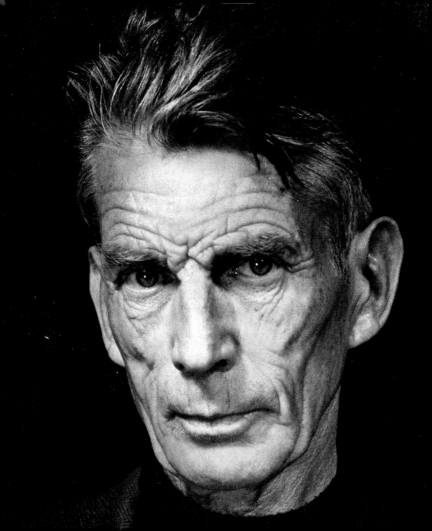

Romantic unhappiness and ill-health contrived to make the next few years of his life difficult. He continued to write, but it was more and more of a challenge. When his permit to stay in Paris expired, he returned to Dublin. His father's sudden death in June 1933 was a blow. He moved to London with a small inheritance and began a course of psychotherapy. He began to have some success with his writing – *More Pricks Than Kicks* was published in 1934 and he was also writing reviews and essays. He had been studying German for several years and in 1936 he decided to go on an artistic tour of Germany, which left him with an intense loathing of the fascism that had engulfed that country. He returned to Dublin in 1937, but in the face of his mother's determination that he get a proper job he returned to Paris. In December he got word that *Murphy* would be published – one month later he was stabbed on the street and he was hospitalised for some weeks. One of his visitors was the pianist Suzanne Deschevaux-Dumesnil – a relationship between them blossomed, although they didn't marry until 1961. Although Beckett had other romantic liaisons, the couple stayed together until her death in 1989.

The Second World War was declared while Beckett was in Dublin visiting his mother. He immediately returned to France, leaving Paris for the countryside with Suzanne. Three months later they returned to Paris, where he worked on a translation of *Murphy*, and he and Suzanne joined the resistance movement. Their cell was betrayed and they fled to the Vaucluse in the unoccupied zone where Beckett worked in the fields. He later received the Croix de Guerre and the Médaille de la Reconnaissance Française in recognition of his service to the French Republic.

When the war was over, he and Suzanne returned to Paris. Their apartment had not been damaged, but the couple had little money in the years after the war. Inflation had reduced the value of his inheritance – to make ends meet, he did translation work and she did dressmaking and gave music lessons. He continued to write, with some success, but everything changed after the opening night of his play *En Attendant Godot* on 3 January 1953. It made him famous almost instantly, and went on to become a hit in Germany, London and New York.

Beckett's mother had died in 1950 and he had inherited enough to build a house outside Paris, which was where he did all his subsequent work. The success of *Godot* meant that he was financially secure, but it made him a public figure in ways that impinged on his time and energies. He spent a lot of time in Paris, giving interviews, attending receptions and generally making himself available, and all the while he went on working. Writing in both English and French, which then proved difficult to translate, he began to turn more and more to theatrical work.

He was awarded the Nobel Prize for Literature in 1969. He regarded this as a disaster and accepted the award on behalf of James Joyce, in his view a more worthy recipient. He gave most of the prize money away.

From the mid-1960s he had suffered ill-health and Suzanne was also unwell. They started wintering in the Mediterranean in order to recuperate without the distractions of their life in Paris. His health disimproved further in the 1980s – he had an enlarged prostate and was diagnosed with Dupuytren's contracture – and began to fail in earnest in 1986 when he developed emphysema and continued to smoke. Suzanne died on 17 July 1989, and Beckett died six months later, on 22 December.

Both during his life and after his death, Beckett received many honours, including honorary doctorates; as an excellent cricketer he had an entry in Wisden, the only Nobel laureate to be included in the cricketer's almanac. His native Ireland has showered with honours of all types. He was elected a Saoi of Aosdána in 1984. An Post issued a commemorative stamp in 1994, and two centenary limited edition coins were issued on 26 April 2006. On 10 December 2009 the Samuel Beckett Bridge over the Liffey was officially opened, and the Irish Navy's LÉ *Samuel Beckett* was named in his honour. He has a blue plaque at the Portora Royal School in Enniskillen, and 2011 saw the inauguration of the first annual Enniskillen International Beckett Festival.

Quotes

Dublin University contains the cream of Ireland: Rich and thick.

There's man all over for you, blaming on his boots the fault of his feet.

The essential doesn't change.

What do I know of man's destiny? I could tell you more about radishes.

All life long, the same questions, the same answers.

I have my faults, but changing my tune is not one of them.

Any fool can turn a blind eye but who knows what the ostrich sees in the sand.

Dance first. Think later. It's the natural order.

How hideous is the semicolon.

Europeans have depth but not distance, while North Americans have distance but not depth.

Words are the clothes thoughts wear.

There are only two moments worthwhile in writing; the one when you start and the other when you throw it into the wastepaper bin.

What was God doing with himself before the creation?

When you're in the shit up to your neck, there's nothing left to do but sing.

What is that unforgettable line?

The mistake one makes is to speak to people.

Probably nothing in the world arouses more false hopes than the first four hours of a diet.

Do you believe in the life to come? Mine was always that.

Every word is like an unnecessary stain on silence and nothingness.

All has not been said and never will be.

Habit is a great deadener.

You're on Earth. There's no cure for that.

Dance first. Think later. It's the natural order

I am still alive then. That may come in useful.

Better hope deferred than none.

Every word is like an unnecessary stain on silence and nothingness.

The tears of the world are a constant quality. For each one who begins to weep, somewhere else another stops. The same is true of the laugh.

Seán O'Casey 1880–1964

All the world's a stage and most of us are desperately unrehearsed.

The dramatist Seán O'Casey was born in Upper Dorset Street in Dublin's inner city on 30 March 1880, into the lower middle-class Protestant family of Michael and Susan Archer. His birth name was John Casey. In 1886 his father died, leaving 13 children. The family's fortunes drifted increasingly downwards as they moved from one house to another on Dublin's north side. O'Casey had hardly any formal education and his eyesight was poor – even so, he taught himself to read and write. He finished with education at the age of 14 and had several jobs, including working for the railway and for Eason's newspaper distribution.

The young O'Casey was interested in drama from an early age, staging Shakespeare and Boucicault plays at home. He even had a small role in Boucicault's *The Shaughraun* in the Mechanics' Theatre in Dublin's Lower Abbey Street, the site of the future national theatre, the Abbey.

He became disenchanted with religion and left the Protestant
Church of Ireland in 1906. Like many others at this time, O'Casey
had an interest in all things to do with Irish nationhood. He joined
the Gaelic League in 1906, learned Irish and changed his name from
John Casey to Seán Ó Cathasaigh, which he later transliterated to the
more Anglophone-friendly 'O'Casey'. With all the energy and zeal of

youth for revolutionary politics, he joined numerous organisations and causes, including the Irish Republican Brotherhood, the Irish Transport and General Workers Union founded by Jim Larkin, and the Irish Citizen Army.

Always true to his roots in Dublin's inner city, he began to lean more towards socialism. He had worked as a labourer for the Great Northern Railway of Ireland, but was dismissed in 1911 when he joined the ITGWU. He raised funds for railway workers and their families during the six-month 1913 Lockout, the rail owners' response to industrial agitation by the ITGWU. He began writing in earnest, turning out pamphlets and songs, and contributing articles and a regular column to the *Irish Worker*.

His love of drama, nurtured in his childhood and youth, had never left him and he was soon concentrating his energies on writing plays. The first to be accepted by the now well-established Abbey Theatre was *The Shadow of a Gunman*, first performed in 1923. Now part of the theatre's stock repertoire, it is a comedy set against the background of revolution. In 1924, the Abbey staged O'Casey's

Juno and the Paycock, followed by *The Plough and the Stars* in 1926. This third play in his so-called Dublin Trilogy provoked riots in the theatre when the audience interpreted the play as an attack on the men of the 1916 Rising. There was also some opposition to the appearance of a prostitute in the second act. W. B. Yeats, one of the directors of the theatre, defused the situation when he told the protesters that they were simply 'shaming themselves'.

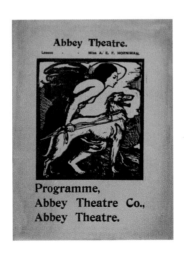

Programme, Abbey Theatre Co., Abbey Theatre.

The notoriety attendant on the play had the positive effect of increasing the box office takings, and O'Casey was finally able to give up his day job and devote himself to writing full time. He was beginning to achieve recognition beyond Ireland's shores and in 1926 he travelled to England to receive the Hawthornden Prize for *Juno and the Paycock* and to supervise a West End production of the play. He met the actress Eileen Reynolds Carey, who was cast in the play, and they were married in 1927. The couple had three children.

Although O'Casey's plays had helped cement the reputation of the Abbey Theatre, his next play, the anti-war, anti-imperialist *The Silver Tassie*, was rejected by the Abbey in 1928, and he decided not to return to Dublin. The play and its rejection became something of a cause célèbre when O'Casey sent the Abbey correspondence to the London newspapers and *The Silver Tassie* was staged in London the following year.

More plays followed, including *Within the Gates* (1934), the anti-fascist *The Star Turns Red* (1940) and *Red Roses for Me* (1946), which was set in Dublin during the 1913 Lockout. However, O'Casey's defining body of work is the Dublin Trilogy. All three plays are tragicomedies set in Dublin's inner-city slums against the backdrop of revolution. The dialogue is sharp and witty and this, more than anything else, has ensured their perennial popularity. None of his later plays achieved anything like the same success.

In the 1930s O'Casey was much in demand as a university lecturer in Britain and America and was a prolific correspondent with the newspapers. He wrote a huge autobiography and a series of articles about the theatre. In 1949 his collected plays were published. His socialist beliefs deepened during the era of fascism, and he was blacklisted as a 'dangerous subversive' during the McCarthy era in the US. In response to Catholic Church censorship of the arts he banned further productions of his work in Ireland.

On 18 September 1964 he died following a heart attack and he was cremated in England. Eileen survived him by more than 30 years.

O'Casey declined numerous awards during his lifetime – the OBE and honorary degrees from the Universities of Durham, Exeter and Trinity College Dublin. In 2005 a footbridge over the River Liffey in Dublin, named in his honour, was opened, and a heritage plaque was erected on his home in East Wall in 2014.

Quotes

It's my rule never to lose me temper until it would be dethrimental to keep it.

———————————

I am going where life is more like life than it is here.

There is none to tell the rich to go on striving, for a rich man makes the law that hallows and hollows his own life.

———————————

Every action of our lives touches on some chord that will vibrate in eternity.

Laughter is wine for the soul – laughter soft, or loud and deep, tinged through with seriousness. Comedy and tragedy step through life together, arm in arm, all along, out along, down along lea. A laugh is a great natural stimulator, a pushful entry into life; and once we can laugh, we can live. It is the hilarious declaration made by man that life is worth living.

You cannot put a rope around the neck of an idea; you cannot put an idea up against the barrack-square wall and riddle it with bullets; you cannot confine it in the strongest prison cell your slaves could ever build.

I never heard him cursing; I don't believe he was ever drunk in his life – sure he's not like a Christian at all.

The flame from the angel's sword in the garden of Eden has been catalysed into the atom bomb; God's thunderbolt became blunted, so man's thunderbolt has become the steel star of destruction.

William Butler Yeats 1865–1939

Being Irish, he had an abiding sense of tragedy, which sustained him thorough temporary periods of joy.

William Butler Yeats was born on 13 June 1865 in Sandymount, County Dublin. His father, John Butler Yeats, was a painter, as was William's brother, Jack Yeats, and his two sisters, affectionately known as Lollie and Lily, were involved in the Arts and Crafts movement. Descended from the Anglo-Norman Butlers of Ormond, Yeats belonged to the Anglo-Irish Protestant minority that had ruled Ireland for several centuries. Yeats was always enthusiastic about his Irish nationality.

The family moved to London when he was still a toddler, and he spent the next 14 years there. The Yeats children were educated at home by their parents for several years, but William was sent to Godolphin School at the age of 11. Now a highly regarded girls' school, in Yeats's day it was regarded as being of little merit. Yeats later said it had 'the rough manners of a cheap school', whose pupils were the sons of failures. He certainly failed to distinguish himself academically, and a report described him as 'very poor in spelling'.

The family returned to Dublin in 1880, first to Harold's Cross, later moving to Howth. The young Yeats spent a lot of time at his father's studio, mixing with artists and writers. He studied at the Metropolitan School of Art from 1884 to 1886, and it was at this time he began writing poetry. His first works were published in *The Dublin University Review* in 1885, dreamy poems that were heavily influenced by the poetry of Shelley and the pre-Raphaelites.

The family went back to London in 1887, and in 1890 Yeats, always drawn to mysticism and spirituality, joined the Hermetic Order of the Golden Dawn, a secret society given to the practice of magic. He remained a member for 32 years, aspiring to the rank of 'magus'. In the same year, more practically, he became one of the founding members of the Rhymers' Club, which, as its name implies, was a forum for poets for the discussion of their work. The club's insistence on rhythm, cadence, form and style would influence Yeats's work for the rest of his life.

During the dying years of the 19th century, Yeats developed an interest in the theatre, an interest that had been nurtured by his father. In 1897 he began an artistic liaison with Lady Augusta Gregory at Coole Park in Galway. In 1899 they began staging three Irish theatrical productions annually, including his own play, *The Countess Kathleen*. This endeavour was so well received that funding to renovate Dublin's Abbey Theatre as a national theatre was procured. The three directors were Yeats, Lady Gregory and J. M. Synge and the theatre opened in December 1904. Yeats, as president, was very involved in the management of the theatre, choosing plays

(famously rejecting George Bernard Shaw's *John Bull's Other Island*), casting and organising for the company to go on tour. During 15 years' involvement in the Abbey, he also wrote a significant number of plays, a development that would affect the style of his poetry, imbuing it with a simplicity that was far more 20th century than 19th, and alienating some readers, who preferred the lyric beauty of poems such as 'Aedh Wishes for the Cloths of Heaven' and the one that everyone knows, 'The Lake Isle of Innisfree'.

In 1889 Yeats met Maud Gonne. It was something of a *coup de foudre* for him and he became obsessed with everything about her. Initially, Gonne had sought out Yeats to compliment him on 'The Island of Statues', his first significant poem.

Gonne was an active Irish nationalist, something that didn't appeal to Yeats at the time (he would change his views in the aftermath of the 1916 Rising). Despite this, he proposed to her in 1891, and again in 1899, 1900 and 1901. She refused him each time and married Major John MacBride in 1903, a move that upset Yeats, who didn't like MacBride and abhorred his politics. The marriage was not successful and Yeats began to visit Gonne in Paris after she and MacBride had been legally separated (MacBride was executed by the British in 1916 for his part in the Rising). Their relationship, however, went nowhere. When he proposed, one last time, she refused and his thoughts turned to her 21-year-old daughter Iseult. He proposed to her in 1917 and was refused, and later that year, he married Georgiana 'George' Hyde-Lees, who was 25 to his 48. He must have felt a need to marry and produce and heir: 'Although I have come close on forty-nine, I have no child, I have nothing but a book,' he wrote.

The marriage was a happy one, despite the disparity in age, and they had a daughter and a son, Anne and Michael. Both Yeats and George had an interest in the occult, and experimented with automatic writing and séances in the early years of their marriage. The spirit communications they received were gathered by Yeats in a book called *A Vision*, published in 1925. Yeats himself regarded it as his 'book of books'.

In 1922, Yeats, who backed the government side in the Civil War, was appointed to the upper house of the Irish parliament, Seanad Éireann, a position he accepted even though members of that government ran the risk of attack and assassination. He was an outspoken opponent of the connection between the state and the Catholic Church, which he believed divisive and an insurmountable obstacle to the inclusion of Northern Ireland in the Republic. Ill health forced his retirement from the Senate in 1928.

In 1923 Yeats was awarded the Nobel Prize for Literature for his poetry, 'which … gives expression to the spirit of a whole nation'. Keenly aware of the symbolism of an Irish laureate in the early days of Irish independence, he always emphasised that the award was intended to honour Irish literature, rather than himself as an individual. Sales of his books rocketed and Yeats was in the unusual position of having money. He was able to pay off his own debts, and those of his father, who always seemed to be in financial difficulty.

In 1934, a vasectomy 'rejuvenated' him (this was then one of the advertised outcomes of the procedure, known as a Steinach operation), and he embarked on a number of romantic affairs, which seem to have had the effect of stimulating his writing.

Even as a young man, Yeats had written about old age and greyness. Now he had reached that point himself. He died at Menton in France in 28 January 1939, and was buried there. In 1948 his remains were moved to Drumcliff in County Sligo, where they were re-interred.

There are unusual statues of the poet in St Stephen's Green, Dublin (Henry Moore, 1967), and in Stephen Street, Sligo (Rowan Gillespie, 1989).

There are plans to turn Toor Ballylee, the Norman keep that was this family's summer home in south Galway, into a cultural centre.

> I, the poet William Yeats,
> With old mill boards and sea-green slates,
> And smithy work from the Gort forge,
> Restored this tower for my wife George.
> And may these characters remain
> When all is ruin once again.

Quotes

There are no strangers here; only friends you haven't yet met.

Was there ever a dog that praised his fleas?

I am of a healthy long-lived race and our minds improve with age.

In dreams begin responsibility.

If the English could only learn to believe in fairies, there wouldn't ever have been any Irish problem.

All empty souls tend towards extreme opinions.

The innocent and the beautiful have no enemy but time.

One should not lose one's temper unless one is certain of getting more and more angry at the end.

She has an ego like a raging tooth.

If suffering brings wisdom, I would wish to be less wise.

Do not wait to strike till the iron is hot – but make it hot by striking.

I am not feeling very well today. I can only write prose.

List of illustrations and picture credits

p3 *W. B. Yeats,* Alice Boughton,1903

p4 *Historical Geography. 1900. Ireland. Old Irish couple off to Galway market.* Bridgeman Images

p5 *A Sick Call,* Matthew James Lawless, 1863, NGI

p10-11 *Samuel Beckett,* unknown

p14-15 Shutterstock, Aitormmfoto

p17 *Portrait of a Child,* 19th century, Irish School, NGI

p18 *An Advice,* Jack Butler Yeats, Creative Commons

p21 *The Irish Whiskey Still,* David Wilkie, Wikiart

p25 *Brendan Behan,* Peter Keen, mid 1950s © estate of Peter Keen / National Portrait Gallery, London

p29 *The Village School,* Jan Steen, c.1665, NGI

p32 *John Philpot Curran,* Unknown artist, National Portrait Gallery, London

p34 *Brehon Law,* Wikipedia

p36 *Woman Washing Clothes,* Francis 'Fanny' Wilmot Currey, 1879, NGI

p41 *The Return of the Prodigal Son,* Pompeo Batoni, 1773, Wikiart

p45 *Print of Irish Leaders,* Library of Congress

p47 Postcard, Teapot Press

p55 *Horse Racing,* Irish Horse Museum

p57 *Donnybrook Fair,* Charles Hunt, 1896, Dahesh Museum of Art, New York, USA / Bridgeman Images

p62 Untitled print, London, 1909, Teapot Press

p65 *Le Mal de Tête,* Honore Daumier, 1833, San Diego Museum of Art / Bridgeman Images

p64-65 Patryk Kosmider / Shutterstock

p73 *Lady Gregory,* Wikipedia

p77 *Oscar Wilde and Lord Alfred Douglas,* Wikipedia

p79 Postcard, Teapot Press

p81 *Thomas Moore,* after Thomas Lawrence, Wikipedia

p82 *Pilgrims at Saint Brigid's Well, Liscannor, County Clare,* George Petrie, 1829-30, NGI

p85 *The Flower Girl,* Henry Gillard Glindoni, 19th century, Bridgeman Images

p87 Victorian print, Wikipedia

p92 *Cupid and Psyche in the Nuptial Boswer,* Hugh Douglas Hamilton, NGI p93 *Two Lovers in a Landscape,* Thomas Bridgeford, 19th century, NGI

p99 *Historical Geography. 1900. Ireland. Old Irish couple off to Galway market,* Bridgeman Images

p102–103 Patryck Kosmider, Shutterstock

p108 *The Foot Doctor,* Adriaen Brouwer, 17th century, NGI

p110 Postcard, Teapot Press

p111 *The Devil's Glen,* print, 1905, Teapot Press

p112 *A Sick Call,* Matthew James Lawless, 1863, NGI

p114 *Frontispiece to Dr Bellendenus's Sermon,* F. W. Fairholt, 19th century, National Library of Ireland

p117 Kletr, Shutterstock

p119 *St. Peter,* Shutterstock, Atila Jandi

p121 Cartoonresource, Shutterstock

p122 Oleg Golonev, Shutterstock

p125 Wikipedia

p127 Vanderwolf, Shutterstock

p131 Francesco de Marco, Shutterstock

p133 *Detail from McCarthy's Wake (Part 1),* 1899 (stereograph), American School, (19th century) / Private Collection / Prismatic Pictures / Bridgeman Images

p135 Krivosheev Vitaly

p137 *Samuel Beckett,* Catwalker, Shuttersrtock

p139 *Irish Funeral* (chalk and pencil), Doyle, John (H. B.) (1797–1868) / © University of Dundee, Scotland, UK / Bridgeman Images

p144–145 *At the graveside during a funeral,* c.1910 (gelatin silver print) Christine Chichester c.1910, Bridgeman Images

p147 Fulcanelli, Bridgeman Images

p148–149 RTÉ / Wikipedia / Wikipedia / Everett Historical, Shutterstock / Everett Historical, Shutterstock

p151 *Brendan Behan in Jackie Gleason's dressing room,* 1960, New York World-Telegram and the Sun staff photographer: Walter Albertin, Library of Congress

p155 Brendan Behan (b/w photo), Jones, Oswald (1929-98) / Private Collection / © Estate of Oswald Jones / Bridgeman Images

p158 *Brendan Behan holding forth in a public house in Blackheath, London,* private collection, RTÉ

p162 *George Bernard Shaw,* Wikipedia

p166 *George Bernard Shaw,* Wikipedia